THE BIBLE AND PATRIARCHY
IN TRADITIONAL TRIBAL SOCIETY

THE BIBLE AND PATRIARCHY IN TRADITIONAL TRIBAL SOCIETY

RE-READING THE BIBLE'S CREATION STORIES

Chingboi Guite Phaipi

LONDON • NEW YORK • OXFORD • NEW DELHI • SYDNEY

T&T CLARK
Bloomsbury Publishing Plc
50 Bedford Square, London, WC1B 3DP, UK
1385 Broadway, New York, NY 10018, USA
29 Earlsfort Terrace, Dublin 2, Ireland

BLOOMSBURY, T&T CLARK and the T&T Clark logo
are trademarks of Bloomsbury Publishing Plc

First published in Great Britain 2023
This paperback edition published 2024

Copyright © Chingboi Guite Phaipi, 2023

Chingboi Guite Phaipi has asserted her right under the Copyright, Designs and Patents Act, 1988, to be identified as Author of this work.

For legal purposes the Acknowledgements on pp. ix-x constitute an extension of this copyright page.

Cover design: Charlotte James
Cover image © Imagezoo/Getty Images

All rights reserved. No part of this publication may be reproduced or transmitted in any form or by any means, electronic or mechanical, including photocopying, recording, or any information storage or retrieval system, without prior permission in writing from the publishers.

Bloomsbury Publishing Plc does not have any control over, or responsibility for, any third-party websites referred to or in this book. All internet addresses given in this book were correct at the time of going to press. The author and publisher regret any inconvenience caused if addresses have changed or sites have ceased to exist, but can accept no responsibility for any such changes.

A catalogue record for this book is available from the British Library.

A catalog record for this book is available from the Library of Congress.

ISBN: HB: 978-0-5677-0766-6
PB: 978-0-5677-0770-3
ePDF: 978-0-5677-0767-3
eBook: 978-0-5677-0769-7

Typeset by Trans.form.ed SAS

To find out more about our authors and books visit www.bloomsbury.com and sign up for our newsletters.

*To my husband, Nengsuanthang Phaipi,
our daughters Chingnunhoih, Lianjarzou, Lunsiang
and our son Liansianmuang.
For our togetherness.*

Contents

Acknowledgments	ix
Abbreviations	xi
INTRODUCTION	1
Scope and Hope of this Book	3
Chapter 1	
PRE-CHRISTIAN TRADITIONAL TRIBAL COMMUNITIES	6
Introduction	6
Was Tribal Women's Subordination in the Pre-Christian Era That Bad?	8
Defining Patriarchy and Women's Subordination	11
Subordination of Women in Traditional Tribal Communities	14
The Paite Tribe: An Introduction	19
Northeast India: A Brief Overview	24
Conclusion	27
Chapter 2	
TRADITIONAL COMMUNITIES AND CHRISTIANITY	28
Introduction	28
Women's Subordination and Christianity	29
The Coming of Christianity to Northeast India	32
Impacts of Christianity on Northeast Indian Tribes	40
Continuities Between Pre-Christianity and the Advent of Christianity	47
Why Are Women Still Subjugated After Embracing Christianity?	48
The Place and View of the Bible in Tribal Christian Society	54
Conclusion	60
Chapter 3	
CREATION OF HUMANITY IN GENESIS 1	62
Introduction	62
Purpose in Creation Account of Genesis 1	64
Creation of Male and Female in God's Image (Genesis 1:26-28)	70
Conclusion	77

Chapter 4
CREATION OF THE FIRST HUMANS IN GENESIS 2 79
   Introduction 79
   Meaning of the Phrase *'ēzer kĕnegdô* 80
   Creation of the *'ēzer kĕnegdô* (Genesis 2:19-23) 84
   Meeting of the Man and the Woman (Genesis 2:23-24) 86
   Conclusion 91

Chapter 5
FIRST MAN AND WOMAN TOGETHER IN THE GARDEN (GENESIS 3) 93
   Introduction 93
   Man with Woman in Disobeying God's Command (Genesis 3:1-12) 94
   Judgment on the Woman (Genesis 3:16) 96
   Judgment on the Man (Genesis 3:17-19) 105
   Conclusion 106

Chapter 6
TOWARD A TRIBAL BIBLICAL HERMENEUTIC 108
   The Need for Tribal Hermeneutics 111
   How Then Shall We Read the Bible? 116

Bibliography 129
Index of References 134
Index of Authors 138

Acknowledgments

This book is born out of my community. My community of friends, families, church, academia, through our informal and formal sharing of our experiences, challenges, and questions, our admiration of the Bible and our culture, and our quest for meaningful connections between the Bible and our lives, have birthed this book. This book is for all the women, men, boys and girls as we continue in our quest to be faithful scriptural people who treasure our rich heritage and culture.

Several people have been crucial in materializing the many conversations and research and plotting out the direction and shape of this book. Rob (Robert) Worley, my friend, mentor and supervisor, and Ted (Theodore) Hiebert, my mentor and colleague in Old Testament/Genesis studies, have gracefully journeyed with me since the very sowing of the seed of this idea to develop an article and/or a book so more could engage in this crucial topic. Without their support, asking hard questions on my drafts and making honest comments, I would not have been able to accomplish this project. My little sister Jennie Ngaihlian in Lamka, Manipur, sacrificed the short breaks she gets between her teaching classes to browse in her college library or run to other places to search for books and other resources for me. These were singularly crucial resources I needed to help others understand my specific context of the Paite tribe in Northeast India. I am deeply thankful to all families, friends, and colleagues, who furnished me with resources, and all those who responded my survey questions, including those whom I do not know in person.

This book could also not have been written without the love, support, and sacrifice of my family. I offer my heartfelt thanks and gratitude to my husband, pastor Nengsuanthang Phaipi, our young daughters Chingnunhoih, Lianjarzou and Lunsiang, as well as our newborn son, Liansianmuang, who already adds inspiration and strength for me to pursue concerns that are vital to my own life and that of my community. This book is a result of our continued effort to live out the Christian teaching sincerely in our own lives.

Finally, I am grateful to my editor Dominic Mattos, editorial assistant Lucy Davies and the rest of the team at Bloomsbury T&T Clark who believed in this project and for guiding it into print so that many more can participate in this conversation. Special thanks go to Duncan Burns for his excellent, professional and generous work in refining my manuscript.

Abbreviations

AB	Anchor Bible
BDB	*A Hebrew and English Lexicon of the Old Testament*, ed. Francis Brown, S. R. Driver and Charles A. Briggs. Oxford: Clarendon Press, 1907
Bib	*Biblica*
CBQ	*Catholic Biblical Quarterly*
CEB	Common English Bible
DCH	*The Dictionary of Classical Hebrew*, edited by David J. A. Clines. Sheffield: Sheffield Academic Press, 2001
HTR	*Harvard Theological Review*
ICHR	*Indian Church History Review*
IJT	*Indian Journal of Theology*
JBL	*Journal of Biblical Literature*
JETS	*Journal of the Evangelical Theological Society*
JSOTSup	*Journal for the Study of the Old Testament*, Supplement Series
JSS	*Journal of Semitic Studies*
LXX	Septuagint
NCBC	New Cambridge Bible Commentary
NIB	*New Interpreters Bible*. 12 vols. Nashville: Abingdon, 2003
NIV	New International Version
NKJV	New King James Version
NLT	New Living Translation
NRSV	New Revised Standard Version
OTL	Old Testament Library
TDOT	*Theological Dictionary of the Old Testament*, ed. G. J. Botterweck and H. Ringgren. 15 vols. Grand Rapids: Eerdmans, 1977–2006
VT	*Vetus Testamentum*
WBC	Word Biblical Commentary
WTJ	*Westminster Theological Journal*

Introduction

I never wanted to write on gender or women's subjugation. In our tribal patriarchal Christian society, any gesture that may be perceived as questioning women's subordination is associated with being unspiritual, or even questioning biblical authority. I desired to be (and be seen as) a godly, respectable woman, not as a rebellious one and feared by my people. I still do, sincerely.

As I became a mother of one, two, and now three very curious young daughters, much of my embedded theology, and many of my underlying prejudices about my reading of the Bible began (and continue) to be tested by their sincere questions. Growing up in the United States in an immigrant church that holds on to those patriarchal values that are the core foundations and ingrained aspects of my own life, my daughters, with pure willing hearts to learn, have earnest observations and questions. I have heard them ask such simple-sounding questions as "Why don't the men help around the house?" Our eight-year-old produced an honest, amazed statement after we attended another (evangelical) church: "I didn't know that women can be pastors too. I have never seen one before!" And then there are the many surprisingly profound questions that emerge when reading the Bible together: "Why don't they give the wife's name too? Don't they have any daughters?" How do I answer these sincere and genuinely curious questions in ways truthful to the Scripture, and without simply recycling the explanations that were told to me when I was growing up—interpretations that I absorbed and adopted without sustained consideration. For indeed, I have come to realise that some of the interpretations I learned as a child are culturally painted readings that are not necessarily founded in the biblical text. Even as my husband and I seek to be good, Christian parents, nurturing our children to live faithful, godly lives, how do I bridge the values that formed me within a traditional, patriarchal tribal Christian community, and what our attentive girls will and do observe and experience—namely, that women's subordination is not necessarily the biblical or Christian order that it is often claimed to be.

There is surely a paradox present in the tribal Christianity of Northeast India with which I am familiar, one that bewilders me and many others. On the one hand, there are the prevalent claims that Christianity has elevated the status of tribal women. On the other hand, there is the fact that women's status and role in the church have not improved, even after a century of Christian missionary activity and outreach. More concerning is that women's subordination continues to be preached as "biblical." And then there are the many perplexing lived experiences.

My journey towards deeper study of the Bible has challenged me to grow in knowledge and experience. My voyage has involved a physical journey from the Northeast Indian tribal Christian context of my childhood, has seen me engage in training in Southeast Asia, and has latterly involved ministry and seminary work in "the West" (Chicago, USA), culminating in a PhD-level Bible training. Experiencing genuine Christian communities founded on egalitarianism, I recall one critical incident, when, as a college girl, while attending a denominational youth conference, I responded to God's call to dedicate my life to full-time ministry. During this event one of the pastors encouraged us to continue to prayerfully seek clearer direction about our callings. The pastor explained to me and my fellow female participants that, as women, our (future) ministry might involve us becoming a pastor's wife. I clearly remember that this statement struck me as strange, though as a young, innocent girl I was not sure why. In the following years, as I pursued theological training abroad, some of my community members questioned why I should "waste" my intelligence doing theological study when I could get a good, secular job and live a fulfilling "normal" life. The well-intentioned advice was that, were I to seek a role in ministry, my destination was inevitable—I would end up like this or that woman, "lost" with no proper ministry, useless and almost certainly unmarried.

The truth is that, within the tribal society in which I was raised, women face more rigid restrictions in the church than in wider society. Whereas women can (now) soar in their professions and careers, within the church women's opportunities are much more limited and constrained. After over a century of Christian mission in Northeast India, women remain excluded from any ministry opportunities as pastors or leaders—except within women-only groups—even though a large number of women have earned theological degrees. Many called and gifted women are left with no official ministry option within the church, and so have to accept a role as the wife of a pastor, as a Sunday school teacher or as a missionary, regardless of whether or not that is their actual calling. And when a called and gifted woman ends up "estranged and astray," she is then quickly judged by the church as not being true to her faith.

There is a clear tension between biblical values and the practices of the tribal patriarchy in which I was raised. While preaching and claiming how in God's eyes and in today's generation male and female are the same/equal, my people also place great importance on having male children. A few years back, when my husband and I were expecting our first child, our tribal community frequently asked if we were having a son. In fact, some did not even ask, they just asserted that we were (they meant, "should be") having a son. We were told by many of our people that it will be a boy—i.e. that it *had better be* a boy—and they prayed for us to have a son. And once people found out that we were having a girl, they would say, in a comforting tone, "Well, boys and girls are the same, the most important thing is that they will grow healthy." I relate this story not to criticize those individuals who proclaimed, wished and prayed for us to have sons—my husband and I also desired the opportunity to raise both girls and boys. I share this encounter, common to many, only to show how our tribal society still values and seemingly "prefers" males over females. These comments are not the result of individual opinions or preferences, but are rather the symptom of an embedded bias within our society that places males at the center and views females as subordinate.

The present work was birthed by ongoing, paradoxical claims and realities such as these. It seeks to address important questions that are raised by the lived experiences of women within tribal Christian communities: Has Christianity indeed impacted positive change in the perception and status of tribal women? Is women's subordination indeed truly biblical?

As I type these words, I still do not think I am writing a book on gender. My sincere wish is more to seek out what is truly biblical and what we confuse as such because of our accepted cultural norms. For me, that is the first step. It is one thing to have women's subordination in our culture, and quite another thing to claim that it is "biblical." In our wish to be a faithful, scriptural people, to be people living in societies shaped by the Bible, deeper and proper study of the Bible and its contexts is the first and essential step. For indeed, what we deem to be "biblical," particularly when it is erroneously and irresponsibly conceived, can and does affect lives and communities adversely.

Scope and Hope of this Book

There are two main aspects to this project. The first is to re-examine the nature and extent of the impact of Christianity on the status of the tribal women of Northeast India, particularly in the Paite tribe. This task is carried out in the first two chapters. Chapter 1 introduces the contexts of the study, namely, the situation of tribal women of Northeast India in the pre-Christian era, focussing in particular on one tribe, the Paite (Zomi). Chapter 2 continues with a survey of the advent of Christianity in Northeast India and the ways in which women's subordination is sustained and reinforced by Christian missionary movements. The chapter also discusses how the Bible is perceived and utilized, at times irresponsibly, to validate tribal cultural norms.

The second aspect of this study is to re-read the biblical creation stories in Genesis 1, 2, and 3. The goal is to examine whether women's subjugation is promulgated in the text. This task is carried out in Chapters 3–5. In Chapter 3 I will demonstrate how the text of Genesis 1 establishes the sameness of male and female in their nature, essence and function by being both created in the image and likeness of God. As I will show, no hierarchy is implied between the male and the female. In Chapter 4 I will re-examine terms and phrases in Genesis 2 that are often used to validate women's subordination, such as the woman being created to be the "helper" of the man. I will elaborate how the terms are not inherently subjugating but rather manifestly pointing towards the partnership between and sameness of the man and the woman. In Chapter 5 I will demonstrate how the text of Genesis 3 contains no indication of the supposed establishment of male authority over females, nor female subordinate status—despite what badly formed interpretations of God's statement, "he will rule over you," might advocate. Finally, in the concluding chapter, after summarizing the findings of the analyses of these two aspects, I will suggest some guidelines for ways to cultivate more faithful readings of the Bible for more responsible applications today.

Genesis 1–3 is chosen for exegesis because these first chapters of the Bible are the most frequently cited texts used to argue for the subordination of women since creation. As it is a genuine desire of the Paite tribal church and society to be faithful to the Scripture, it is crucial to re-examine the biblical narratives closely to avoid eisegesis. Eisegesis is basically reading our culture into the biblical narrative and utilizing the biblical narrative to legitimate our own preconceived ideologies. Such a way of reading the Bible and applying it into our contexts is essentially being unfaithful to the Scripture, and actually contradictory to our desire to live biblically faithful lives.

The intent of this study is not first and foremost to critique tribal societies. Rather, the hope of this study is to bring about a more faithful reading of the Scripture, something which is so important to tribal Christian communities. It is my sincere hope that this study will inspire us not to be too hasty when applying biblical texts to our contexts. I also hope this study will motivate us to offer more careful readings of biblical narratives in their own terms, as well as deeper studies of our own contexts, before drawing out "biblical" stipulations into our lived experiences. Let us now begin our study by setting forth the contextual backgrounds in Chapter 1.

Chapter 1

Pre-Christian Traditional Tribal Communities

Introduction

In Northeast Indian tribal societies, images of women are rather negative, and factors like education, occupation and religion have not succeeded in overcoming gender biases.[1] While men benefitted from the coming of Christianity, with the Church becoming the center of power and patronage through mission agencies employing those young men they had educated to preach and teach, women's status, opportunities and options have remained the same or diminished, particularly within the Church.[2] In spite of many claims that Christianity has elevated tribal women's condition, history and reality show continuing reinforcement of subordination. This fact compels us to re-examine the general assumption that Christianity brought elevation of tribal women's status. In order to re-evaluate Christianity's impact on tribal society, particularly women's situation, it is first essential to study the life and society of the tribes before the coming of Christianity. This task will be undertaken in this chapter, followed by a study of the advent of Christianity in the next chapter. While most tribal women in Northeast India share the same fate, this study will focus on one Northeast Indian tribe, the Paite (Zomi),[3] with the findings being relevant for other tribes.

---

1. Rose Nembiakkim, *Reproductive Health Awareness Among the Tribal Women in Manipur* (New Delhi: Concept Publishing, 2008), 12.
2. Songram Basumatary, *Ethnicity and Tribal Theology: Problems and Prospects for Peaceful Co-existence in Northeast India* (Oxford: Peter Lang, 2015), 85.
3. About ten tribes belong to the Zomi nomenclature, and all these tribes have the same culture and religion except for slight variations in their dialects. In this book I will use Paite and Zomi interchangeably, particularly when citing resources

Phaipi notes about the Paite tribe: "...before the coming of Christianity the position of women among the Paites was subordinate and oppressive. In fact, most of these oppressive customs are still practiced today."[4] Today, no denomination among the Paite ordains women, and women are excluded from any position of authority and offices like that of ministers or elders, even though a large number of women have been studying theology since the 1980s.[5] The common belief among tribal people is that since the beginning of time, women (from biblical Eve) are limited, prone to being deceived and thus should be controlled or ruled by men. Preachers today take the liberty to validate and promote women's subordination and males' authority over females as biblical and the right spirituality. According to tradition, a Paite woman is believed to have no religion of her own: "she belongs to her natal spiritual group before her marriage...and then after marriage to her husband's ancestral spiritual group."[6] Although this belief would be contested in contemporary Paite society, it remains deeply seated in people's mindsets. For example, while it remains a taboo for Paite women to get married to non-Christians as if her being a Christian will be lost or revoked instantly, a Paite man marrying a non-Christian faces fewer obstacles and is judged less harshly by the society.

Paite women's in-family roles still reflect traditional gender-subordination. In the household council *Inndongta* that controls matters like marriage, birth, death and conflicts, the only position played by women (only by married women), called the *tanute* ("daughters," normally there

---

on Zomi, as it speaks truly and directly about the Paite individual tribe too. The Paite tribe will be introduced in a later section. To read more about the Paite tribe, see H. Kamkhenthang, *The Paite: A Transborder Tribe of India and Burma* (New Delhi: Mittal Publications, 1988).

4. Ashley Nengsuanthang Phaipi, "Mission Transformation for Evangelical Baptist Convention, India: From Evangelistic Approach to Integral Mission" (DMin. diss., Lutheran School of Theology at Chicago, 2018), 19.

5. Tara Manchin Hangzo, "Gender Equality Among the Zomis," in *Democratisation Process in North-East India: Some Issues and Challenges*, ed. S. Thianlalmuan Ngaihte and L. T. Sasang Guite (New Delhi: Gyan Publishing House, 2015), 68. The Evangelical Baptist Convention is the largest denomination among the Paite tribe, and has 67,632 members and 209 local churches (according to the 2021 EBC Annual Census). EBC has no women leaders at the local or denominational level, except for one position to be occupied by a woman, known as a "Dorcas Worker" ("Dorcas" being the name given to women's ministry within the wider denomination).

6. H. Kamkhenthang, "Role of Women in the Customary Practices of the Paite," in *Gender Implications of Tribal Customary Law: The Case of North-East India*, ed. Melvil Pereira et al. (New Delhi: Rawat Publications, 2017), 163–4.

are up to three *tanu* in one family council), is to manage domestic tasks. And at *Inndongta* meetings, the reticence of women is seen as ideal behavior in this male-dominated atmosphere.[7] Women are not to speak or voice their opinions; instead, they are to silently obey and carry out the decisions reached by the male members. The Paite elite is also represented solely by males, though Paite women are advancing in the professions and government, and traditional roles endure in religious and community organizations.[8] Among the Paite organizations, only the *Siamsinpawlpi* (students association) has some women participating at a leadership level—but there too, not in decision- and policy-making positions.

These few examples of Paite tribal women still subordinated in the Church and society are contradictory to the common assumption that Christianity has elevated women's situation. It is thus intriguing to examine the situation of women before the coming of Christianity to help understand the nature of the impact of Christianity on tribal women. There is one important preliminary question that needs to be addressed prior to delving into an analysis of pre-Christian-era tribal societies. It is debated whether the situation of women was indeed that bad, and whether it was rather Christianity (and British colonialism) that had suppressed tribal women through their new political and belief systems.

Was Tribal Women's Subordination in the Pre-Christian Era That Bad?

Some authors have noted that Northeast India women had relatively higher status before the arrival of colonialism and Christianity. For instance, Ray argues that the goddesses of Northeast India, unlike those of south India, "did not have any male consort, suggesting that the female element was not subdued."[9] Rodrigues also argues that "the traditional roles ascribed to women garnered them similar respect as the roles ascribed to men," but that their dignity and respect were soon restricted by modern male-dominated institutions in the name of customary laws.[10] In *jhum* economy and communitarian traditions of the tribal economy no property was

---

7. Ibid., 164.
8. S. Thianlalmuan Ngaihte, *Elite, Identity and Politics in Manipur* (New Delhi: Mittal Publications, 2013), 67–8.
9. Asok Kumar Ray, "Tribal Women in North-East India," in Pereira et al., eds, *Gender Implications of Tribal Customary Law*, 48.
10. Shaunna Rodrigues, "Negotiating Equality: Endorsing Women's Rights Through Customary Laws," in Pereira et al., eds, *Gender Implications of Tribal Customary Law*, 71–2.

ever strictly private until the new landlord systems under colonial rule empowered male chiefs. Furthermore, in spite of colonial dominion, some tribes also survived having retained matrilineal cultural practices, such as the Khasi, Garo and Jainta tribes.

In a similar manner, careful consideration offers hints of Paite tribal women being in a better situation in previous periods than is usually accepted. For instance, while it is true that most Paite folklore stereotypes show women as objects of beauty who fulfill male desires and who are in need of male protection,[11] some folklore does paint women as exhibiting certain agency and independence. In the folktale *Khupching leh Ngambawm*, the mother of the girl Khupching successfully obstructs the marriage plan of her daughter and her lover. In another folktale, *Thanghou leh Liandou*, the widow and mother of Thanghou and Liandou leaves her husband's household and two sons to look for another man. It is also significant that the woman, Khupching, is named first in *Khupching leh Ngambawm*, a folktale well known among and shared by many tribes in Northeast India. Some folksongs also imply the necessity of agreement of the women/mothers for marriage.[12]

Another interesting fact that points to the possibly honorable and high status of women is in the worship of female deities. This contrasts markedly with what we find today, where it is unimaginable to associate the feminine with God. Recently, a popular young preacher in a viral social-media post proclaimed that God, *Pathian*, cannot be *Nuthian* ("Pa" is a masculine marker, and "Nu" feminine), warning that associating feminine essence is dangerous, and equivalent to the worship of goddesses/idols. In the pre-Christian era, however *Pisha* (literally "grandma worship") was prominent among the Paites. *Pisha* was the worship of the grandmother of two orphans, Thanghou and Liandou.[13] *Pisha* worship reveals the possible high estimation of females and/or the female deity within the generally assumed context of extremely low regard for females.

---

11. Mercy Vungthianmuang Guite and Grace Donnemching, "Gender Represenetation in Folklore Culture: Dissection of Selected Paite Tribe of Manipur," *Political Economy Journal of India* 26, no. 1 (January–June 2017): 80–6.

12. T. Liankhohau, *Social, Cultural, Economic and Religious Life of a Transformed Community: A Study of Paite Tribe* (New Delhi: Mittal Publications, 1994), 2, 52.

13. *Pisha* worship also seems to be the origin of ancestor worship practiced in pre-Christian Paite society. Overall, *Pisha* worship is mainly associated with blessings for the home and harvest in the field, for a prosperous and healthy life and livelihood at home. Shinkhokam, *Pu-Pa Nun* [Life of Forefathers] (Lamka: Self Published, 2005), 90–3.

It is also worthwhile to consider the fact that the Paite tribe's culture was oral and traditions were passed down through generations orally. With the coming of literacy, the Paite tribe began to keep written records, and oral transmission seemed to rapidly decline. Stories of women's power and agency would have been lost in the transition from oral to written culture, or many stories would possibly have been distorted. For instance, in describing the importance of *pu* (mother's brother) in the requisite institution of every Paite household, *inndongta*, and in Paite culture in general, Kamkhenthang notes that the prominence of the *pu* may be a survival of the earlier matrilineal practices. He affirms, "*Pu* is the most respected member in the *inndongta* as he is from the natal side of the mother… As an honour, he was to drink the best part of the rice-beer."[14] He further points out that the importance of *pu* comes from his married sister, indicating the power of a married woman who empowers her brother and raises his status. As Kamkhenthang concludes, the critical place of a sister/woman is not preserved, documented or has perhaps been distorted. This is highly possible in light of Ray's finding that the colonial ethnographers documented the customary laws through male voices and that they always reflect male interests.[15] That is to say that the exact status of women is hard to recover. Nonetheless, the available evidence suggests that women's situation was not as terrible as we might assume today.

To my mind, the situation of tribal society in general in pre-modern times, thus the pre-Christian era, was simply underdeveloped. In that respect, then, while women's situation was bad, perhaps it was not as bad as usually portrayed today when judged against the background of the standards of that era. In other words, women's subordinated situation then is perhaps not too different from women's subordinated situation today, with most women still struggling for their rights and freedom and mostly under male domination. It becomes a critical question, then, whether women have really been elevated from their pre-Christian-era situation by the advent of Christianity, with respect to the wider contemporary historical background.

Weighing the meager yet significant evidence we have, the following conclusion can be made: there is evidence of women's agency, though it does not seem that women in general had higher or equal status to men. At the least, it needs to be acknowledged, not overlooked, that women in pre-Christian times were not totally subjugated, even within their patriarchal society, at least not in all aspects of society or home. This is a more

---

14. Kamkhenthang, "Role of Women in the Customary Practices," 163.
15. Ray, "Tribal Women in North-East India," 50.

truthful portrayal of the broader situation of pre-Christian tribal societies such as the Paite. This finding confirms the relevance and necessity of the question whether and how the Christian missions impacted women's status. It also raises the question whether the Paite tribe was really patriarchal. A definition of patriarchy is called for.

Defining Patriarchy and Women's Subordination

The term "patriarchy" literally means "rule of father," from the Greek *pater* and *archē*. Based on this literal, basic meaning, patriarchy has been widely used to describe societies, both ancient and contemporary. Recently, however, problems, inadequacies and inaccuracies of employing the term "patriarchy" to define societies, particularly ancient, have been raised. For instance, Miller concedes that models such as patriarchy could not capture the factual social order of the complex past societies, and therefore rather resorts to surveying the benefits and drawbacks of how the term patriarchy has been used as a conceptual word in history.[16] Similarly, Meyers points out the problems of utilizing the term patriarchy particularly for ancient society such as biblical Israel. She notes that the term is based not on biblical theory or content itself but rather comes from later Greek and Roman legal sources as used by nineteenth-century Western anthropologists.[17] Meyers proposed to utilize a model employed by social scientists, *heterarchy*, to better reflect biblical Israel society. According to Meyers, ancient Israel was not strictly patriarchal, but allowed women various forms of agency. Furthermore, rather than being rigidly hierarchical, male–female relationships were more interdependent and mutual.[18] Fiorenza also describes ancient biblical societies (and some contemporary cultures in various settings) in terms of *kyriarchy*, a term which she feels better reflects the intersectionality of domination.[19]

---

16. Pavla Miller, *Patriarchy* (New York: Routledge, 2017).

17. Carol Meyers, "Gender and the Heterarchy Alternative for Re-Modeling Ancient Israel," in *The Oxford Handbook of Feminist Approaches to the Hebrew Bible*, ed. Susanne Scholz (Oxford: Oxford University Press, 2020), 443–59.

18. Carol Meyers, "Hierarchy or Heterarchy? Archaeology and the Theorizing of Israelite Society," in *Confronting the Past: Archaeological and Historical Essays in Honor of William G. Dever*, ed. Seymour Gitin, J. P. Dessel, and J. Edward Wright (Winona Lake: Eisenbrauns: 2006), 249–51.

19. *Kyriarchy* comes from the Greek *kyrios* for "lord, master, legal guardian" and *archein* from "to rule, dominate." See Elisabeth Schüssler Fiorenza, "Biblical Interpretation and Kyriarchal Globalization," in Scholz, ed., *The Oxford Handbook of Feminist Approaches to the Hebrew Bible*, 3.

In essence, the main problem of utilizing a term such as patriarchy is that it is notoriously difficult to precisely define the term, with it being used loosely in a wide variety of ways.[20] Indeed, the term "patriarchy" is used variously to speak of the absolute power of a father over family members; to refer to society-wide male dominance; to describe male dominance over all women; to connote a rigid hierarchy based only on a male–female dichotomy and concomitant victimhood of females/women; and to define the everyday experience of legal, systemic and structural operations. And yet it is interesting to note that the very contexts within which the concept of patriarchy supposedly originated—the Greek and Roman households and societies—do not seem to have been absolutely patriarchal in all aspects.[21] Clearly, patriarchalism has been defined and used in a wide variety of ways and yet cannot accurately reflect all the realities of the society it attempts to describe. But, as a matter of fact, no single model can perfectly and fully capture a given society in all of its detailed, complex and real aspects.

Any term and model utilized to represent and describe a society, current or past, is subject to exceptions and questions.[22] As such, on the one hand, I agree with scholars about the complications and inadequacy of utilizing terms such as patriarchy for ancient society as well as modern tribal societies like the Paite. But also, on the other hand, I accept that there is no better term and model for describing a society like that of the Paite. To my mind, "patriarchy" is still the best available term to denote a system, culture or society where the concept and practice of male supremacy is predominant.[23] That being the case, I will use the term patriarchy in the present study where necessary.

Essentially, the term "patriarchy" will be used in this book to describe a society where male authority and perspectives are viewed and accepted to be the ultimate norm both at home and in public settings; a society

---

20. Both Miller and Meyers provide helpful surveys of how varied the term has been used in history, religion, politics, feminist and liberation critiques and so on. See Miller, *Patriarchy*; Meyers, "Gender and the Heterarchy Alternative," 443–59.

21. Meyers, "Gender and the Heterarchy Alternative," 447–50.

22. For example, even if we employ *heterarchy* as a model, it is still not without drawbacks and questions. For instance, how is the agency distributed among the gender? Is agency still predominantly male, with sporadic opportunities for women? Is it different across class, age, home and public, urban or rural, political or religious settings? Other questions are still to emerge.

23. Judith M. Bennett, *History Matters: Patriarchy and the Challenge of Feminism* (Philadelphia: University of Pennsylvania Press, 2006), 56.

where male is primary, at the center, and female is secondary, at the periphery. Such is the experience of the members of the Paite society. The Paite society was and is predominantly male-dominated, male-centric and male-preferring, with women in many ways seen as second-class humans. Yet also, as discussed earlier, there were/are exceptions to the norm—of women's agency. So, when the term patriarchy is used, in no way does it indicate an absence of exceptions.

In traditional patriarchal tribal societies like the Paite's, the interests of males are at the center, and male authority and perspectives are the norm. For example, a woman perceived as controlling a man earns a very negative estimation, while a man able to control woman/women is highly regarded; conversely, a man not controlling woman is seen as weak and not manly enough. A man whose wife is financially more successful than him is often ridiculed, implying his wife's success threatens his manhood and that it may be hard to exercise his authority over her.[24] Principally, the idea that men are superior to women is the norm, one promoted in virtually all areas of the society, from the basic unit—the home and family—to religious institutions such as the Church and all other social organizations. A "well functioning" patriarchal society is one in which the men of a society define, through religious teachings, customs and traditions and laws, from male-centered perspectives, what is and should be the norm in the society. It is in this sense that the term "patriarchy" will be used in this book.

Let me be clear here: "patriarchy" is not to be equated to "men," especially when it is critiqued. Critiquing patriarchy is not about blaming men and victimizing women. In fact, most women in traditional tribal society such as the Paite's support patriarchy—they raise their sons and daughters to conform to it. Also, throughout the history of patriarchy, not all men have gained equally from patriarchal structures. In some contexts some women may even enjoy privileges that some men do not.[25] Nonetheless, even when women seem to accomplish more than men, it is *in spite of* being a woman, by being able to do what men do in the way men do. All in all, when considered as a group, women were/are disempowered compared to the men, as a group, of the same society.

---

24. These illustrations are parallel with what Johnson gives to explain how male control and fear are central in (any) patriarchal society. See Allan G. Johnson, *The Gender Knot: Unraveling Our Patriarchal Legacy*, 3rd ed. (Philadelphia: Temple University Press, 2014), 14–15, 56.

25. Bennett, *History Matters*, 56–7.

Another related term that will be used—in fact more frequently than "patriarchy"—is "women's subordination," a term that more precisely expresses the focus and interest of this study. Subordination of women is one of the direct effects and manifestations of patriarchy. The term "women's subordination," as used in this study, is a reference to the situation in which women are viewed as secondary to men in essence and value, and thereby restricts them to certain roles. That is, it is an ontological concept leading to a functional one. Patriarchy and women's subordination are intertwined. As a result of the concept of patriarchy, backed by religious teachings, it is perceived as right and permissible to subjugate women.

We have now laid out the preliminary questions and definitions, and so we now turn to analyze the subordination of women in tribal societies, and to explore how it functioned within such contexts. Importantly, most of the concepts and practices that were subordinating to females continued to be practiced even after Christianity had been embraced. Indeed, they persist even today.

Subordination of Women in Traditional Tribal Communities

The subordination of women within traditional tribal communities of Northeast India works in both overt and covert ways. The patriarchal customary laws and traditions were and continue to be the defining laws that govern the running of tribal societies. Many of these customary laws overtly subordinate women and are still in evidence today. In more subtle ways, there are numerous sayings and expressions, gestures and rituals that live on, ones which express the covert, deep-rooted ideological discrimination and subordination of women. Most Northeast Indian tribal communities share a similar set of customary laws that govern the communities, as well as a stock vernacular sayings that are clearly patriarchal and patronizing towards females. In an effort to shed further light on this, the customary laws of the Paite tribe will now be examined.

Paite Tribal Customary Law and Women

Before the coming of Christianity, the Paites had a well-organized oral tradition, and their life and society were practically governed and controlled by customary laws, proverbs and folk songs.[26] The Paite

---

26. Luai Chin Thang, "A History of the Evangelical Baptist Convention Among the Paite Tribe in North East India" (DMin. diss., Reformed Theological Seminary, Jackson, MS, 2000), 84.

customary laws are self-evidently patriarchal in origin, and a few examples will suffice to show the low status that Paite society afforded women.[27] As we progress with our survey, it will be noticeable that some of the Paite customary laws bear similarities to those of the ancient/biblical Israelites. Those similarities make it easy for Paites to relate to biblical stories, but also at times lead to biblical texts being read only at face value.

The view of women's impermanence is not hard to miss in the Paite customary laws. Consider the dictum: "a woman cannot bring in her parent's traditional practices to her husband's family."[28] That is, the bride shall give up the custom of her parents from the date of marriage, regardless of "whether the bride price is fully paid or not."[29] This dictum means that, until marriage, a woman is bound by her parents' customs; thereafter, she is in turn bound by her husband's customs. In such a situation, it is as if the woman has no customs of her own, but rather borrows and adopts according to her marital status, in which she also has little say. Ideologically, women are seen to be status-less and value-less on their own.

A ceremony that exhibits the dependent status of women is *Putawp Zukholh*, where *pu* is a maternal uncle and *tawp* means "last" or "end." It is a ceremony where tea (rice-beer used to be consumed) is offered to a woman's maternal uncle when she gets married.[30] This ceremony is performed because the woman, following her marriage, "now belongs to her husband's family."[31] Through *Putawp Zukholh*, a married woman closes off her official *Pu*. This ceremony speaks to the view of woman's impermanence, since it is only women who sever this relationship with her *Pu*, while "a man cannot sever his life-long ritual relationship with his mother's brother."[32] Today, this ceremony itself is not strictly carried out

---

27. On February 1, 2002, a Paite Customary Court was instituted to be the highest standing court to decide cases arising within the Paite community. Simultaneously with the establishment of the Paite Customary Court, the Paite Tribe Council published the Paite Customary Laws, which were amended in 2013. The Paite Tribe Court was instituted under the Paite Tribe Council, the highest authority-holding organization of the Paite tribe. To date, the Paite Tribe Council has tried and decided more than 152 cases, out of which 148 cases were settled. Th. Siamkhum, *The Paites: A Study of the Changing Faces of the Community* (Chennai: Notion Press, 2013), 151.

28. Article 20 in *The Paite Customary Law & Practices 2nd Amendment, 2013*.

29. Siamkhum, *The Paites: A Study*, 49.

30. Article 21 (i) in *The Paite Customary Law & Practices 2nd Amendment, 2013*. Siamkhum, *The Paites: A Study*, 158.

31. Siamkhum, *The Paites: A Study*, 158.

32. Kamkhenthang, "Role of Women in the Customary Practices," 163.

by all families, yet the custom that a woman's *Pu* is no longer the official *Pu* is understood, as she adopts her husband's *Pu*.

There is also a similar *Putawp Zukholh* ceremony in the event of the death of a husband. In the case of a death of the head (father) of a family, his children should perform *Putawp Zukholh* to the *Pu Pi* ("main grandfather," that is, the father's father), the deceased's father. This ceremony signifies that the wife's brother will become the *Pu Pi* to his children, and it is also necessary to reconstitute the *Inndongta* (household council) accordingly.[33] This ceremony is basically the transfer of the seat of the main *Pu* of children, which is by default the father's father, to the mother's brother. Now, this may appear to grant some prominence to the mother or the mother's line, but in actuality the mother is merely the channel through which a male member from her former family obtains a seat in the kinship/family unit.

Another ceremony that shows the prominence given to male members is *Langkhen*, which is performed by a maternal uncle (*pu*) when a nephew dies and the uncle conducts the burial ceremony. It is said that "no one [should] bury the dead body in the absence of 'Pute'...and when the maternal uncle performs *Langkhet*, the nephew's brothers feed the deceased's maternal uncle with 'Pu Zutawi'."[34] Significantly, there is no ceremony of *Langkhen* for women, since her parental clansmen already bid her farewell on the day of her marriage, the moment when her soul spirit joined the spiritual band of her husband's group.[35] It is therefore said traditionally that a woman has no permanent religion or permanent place. In addition, if a husband dies without a child, the childless widow is sent back to her *Nolam* on the day of her husband's burial. (*Nolam* literally means "back side"—that is, her original family is her back side after marriage.) While today this custom is not practiced by all families and is used on a case-by-case basis, knowledge of the tradition still reflects the view of women being impermanent and status-less if they do not have a husband or children, especially (a) son(s).

Though the customs just described are not practiced by everyone, the core concepts remain widely acknowledged and typically go unchallenged. An example of a mandatory custom that is still followed today—one that clearly reveals the subordinated status of women—is the paying of the bride price. In Paite tribe customary law, there are two essential prices that must be fulfilled in order for a Paite woman to be recognized as properly married. The first one is called *Tukli leh Thaman*,

33. Siamkhum, *The Paites: A Study*, 159.
34. Ibid.
35. Kamkhenthang, "Role of Women in the Customary Practices," 163.

literally "four-palm sized and wage," which refers to the fee paid to the bride's family by the groom's family in order to acquire the right to bury the woman in the event of her death. To put it crudely, it is the right to own the bride/woman in life as well as death. In the past, the value of a four-palm sized pig is set at rupees four and the wage is set at rupees two but have been increased to rupees two thousand and rupees one thousand respectively.[36] The other essential price that needs to be paid in order for a woman to be married in a proper sense is *Mou Man*, the bride price. Historically, the bride price was spoken of in terms of "mithun," which was the most valuable item of property (typically a domestic animal), and a bride price was generally two mithuns, sometimes referred to as an adult mithun and a calf. Today, the bride price is spoken of in terms of currency and is set at rupees two thousand and one thousand for a mithun and a calf respectively. While these monetary values are much lower than the actual market value of appropriate-sized pig or mithuns and wage, they are set by a philanthropic organization at such a level that all families, especially poor families, can pay. It may be mentioned here that the payment of "prices" in marriage customs are one of the areas where the Paite tribe shares a similarity with ancient Israelite tribal customs. However, and importantly, while shared similarities allow a reader to connect easily with the biblical stories, they also at times prevent us from seeing the differences. Significantly, the identification of similarities makes it all too easy for customs to be considered to be the same as ones appearing in the Bible, even when they are not. Furthermore, such similarities potentially blind us to the fact that such customs do not serve well all members of the community.

Today, while it may be challenged that the bride price is not an indication of a woman being "bought" like some kind of commodity, or that the bride price does not signify the woman's "worth," the correlation is deeply seated in people's mindset, particularly among men. It is not uncommon to hear men making statements, either casually in jokes or sometimes in all seriousness, that because they have paid money for their wife, they have total authority over them. In her analysis of the traditional marriage system in the Mizo society, which is similar to that of the Paite, Hminthanzuali convincingly argues that the custom of bride price ensures male hegemony.[37] She argues that the custom confirms that women belong to men, resulting in women, just like a movable assets, being circulated

36. Siamkhum, *The Paites: A Study*, 164.
37. Hminthanzuali, "Bride Price and Patriarchal Hegemony in the Mizo Society," in *Gender Lens: Women's Issues and Perspectives*, ed. Rekha Pande (New Delhi: Rawat Publications, 2015), 383.

in marriage through bride price, a price fixed by the men of the society or family.

Paite customary succession and inheritance laws are also gender based and biased. In regard to succession and inheritance, property, both acquired and inherited, movable and immovable, is to be succeeded by the eldest son. In those instances where "the head of a family has no son at the time of his death…the properties will go to the nearest male member of his relatives."[38] While the customary law also allows a father without a son to distribute his movable and immovable properties to his daughter(s), if no proper distribution or deed (will) was made during his lifetime, "the inheritor" (that is, the nearest male relative) will inherit all his properties.[39] These succession and inheritance laws also look similar to those known from biblical Israel. As such, they are easily perceived and uncritically practiced as though they are biblically sanctioned, regardless of whether or not they function for the welfare of all the community's members.

Unscripted Standards and Women's Subordination
Even more significant in revealing the view of women in the Paite society, as in many other Northeast Indian tribal societies, are the unscripted, subtle yet prevalent gestures, jokes and sayings about women. These sayings are seen in most, if not all, tribes of Northeast India, either in identical or markedly similar statements. These sayings about women reveal how women are viewed as impermanent, incapable and secondary. In Paite society, such sayings include *Numei gilou leh mei-awng kal a nisa*, which translates "A wicked woman and the sun in between clouds"; *Numei pilna in sangkil a kankei*, which translates "The wisdom of women does not cross the door threshold"; and *Numei vak hat thusia zong*, meaning "A woman who loiters around is looking for trouble." Other sayings include "Just as a goat is without teeth, so a woman lacks brain"; "Flesh of a crab is no meat; words of a woman are no words"; and "Women and crabs do not have religious rites."[40] Such sayings about women reveal that women were/still are seen to be unreliable and limited, as if not possessing full human capabilities.

---

38. Article 81 and 82 of *The Paite Customary Law & Practices 2nd Amendment, 2013*. Siamkhum, *The Paites: A Study*, 171.

39. Article 84 of *The Paite Customary Law & Practices 2nd Amendment, 2013*. Siamkhum, *The Paites: A Study*, 171.

40. Shiluinla Jamir, "State, Patriarchy and Gender: Everyday Resistance of Women in the Borderland (Northeast India)," *Religion and Society* 63, no. 1 (2018): 75–6; Hminthanzuali, "Bride Price and Patriarchal Hegemony," 380.

Some other sayings deriving from tribal societies also reflect how women are viewed inhumanely, sometimes serving as warnings about the danger of leaving women uncontrolled. For example, "Men usually prefer to have choice in the selection of guns rather than in girl friends";[41] "Do not pay heed to what a woman says; let a woman and a dog bark as they please"; "Uncontrolled wives and untrimmed grass in the fields both become unbearable"; "Worn out fencing and a woman can be replaced." Even today, sayings such as these are occasionally deployed in casual exchanges or during heated arguments. As such, contemporary mores and gestures offer strong indications of how women are subordinated in tribal societies such as the Paite's. For instance, Paite men actively avoid passing under women's clothes or skirts that are suspended on a clothes-line for fear, though blatantly baseless, that they will be "under" women. Notably, during meetings of mixed groups, men typically take the seats, while women (along with the children) occupy the floor.

The above brief survey shows that the customs and standards in tribal societies view and value women as subordinate. In our interest to understand better the impact of Christianity on Northeast Indian tribes and their women, it is important to explore the broader context—the history, society and culture. This broader understanding will help us situate the position of women in their own background as well as prepare us with an awareness of the overall contexts faced by Christian missionaries as they sought to sow new, Christian, ideologies. Therefore, in the remaining sections of this chapter I will briefly summarize the situation that pertains to the Paite tribe, the principal focus of our study, before moving on to discuss the wider region of Northeast India.

The Paite Tribe: An Introduction

The Paite tribe inhabits Northeast India and belongs to the Zomi people group. Though many Paite and other Zomi tribes now live in diaspora all over the world, they originally and mainly inhabited the Manipur and Mizoram states in Northeast India and the Chin state in Myanmar. The Paite, just like other tribes of Northeast India, trace their historical origin to western China, with the ancestors migrating south through Myanmar and continuing on to the Northeast region of present-day India. The Paite-speaking people claim their historical settlement at Chimnuai in the Chin state of Burma.[42] The term "Paite," which literally means

---

41. Basumatary, *Ethnicity and Tribal Theology*, 60.
42. Kamkhenthang, *The Paite: A Transborder Tribe*, 2.

"goers" (*pai* = go; *te* = plural), denotes their migratory habit, identifying them as people on the move.[43] Formerly known by their clan names such as Guite and Sukte, "Paite" became the term used to refer to the tribe in India since the time of India's independence from the British and the separation of Myanmar from India, whereas "Tedim Chin" is the term used for the same people in Myanmar.[44] The government of India recognized the Paite as one of the Scheduled Tribes of the country in 1956.[45]

Historically, the Paites are divided into clans with two distinct classes, one of chiefs and the other of commoners.[46] The clans in turn are divided into lineages. The main function of the clans is the regulation of properties and providing protection to its members. The Paite tribe, despite being organized into clans, is fundamentally interknitted and community based. At the base of the Paite tribe kinship unit, the individual household, is the traditional Household Council, *Inndongta*, which guarantees kinship obligations and reciprocal co-operation. Through the *Inndongta*, each household is related to other households both through in-clan and non-clan members.[47] For instance, the office of *Thallouh* is held by the nearest patrilineal male member of the father of the household, while the office of *Thusapi* is to be held by a non-clan member of the village; while the office of *Tanu* is held by the married daughter/s of the family, the office of *Zawl* is a trusted friend of the head (father) of the household. *Inndongta* functions as the basic representative of the family, and is the policy- and decision-making body for the household in all matters such as death, marriage and divorce. Most issues related to disputes between different families are handled through traditional *Inndongta* negotiations; when matters are too serious, families appeal to the Paite Customary Court.

The communal nature of the Paite tribe is also observable in their traditional *jhum* economy system. In what was called *Lawm*, "corporate weeding," men and women worked in groups and weeded fields together,

---

43. Ibid., 7.

44. Though the term "Paite" had been in use for a long time, it was officially accepted on record by the people themselves in 1948 with the formation of the Paite National Council. The Paite language was recognized by the government of Manipur as a medium of instruction in primary schools in 1977 and at the high school level in 1989. Today, the Paite language is one of several vernaculars studied at graduate level at Manipur University. Kamkhenthang, *The Paite: A Transborder Tribe*, 8.

45. To read more about Scheduled Tribes of India, see K. S. Singh, *The Scheduled Tribes*, People of India National Series 3 (Delhi: Oxford University Press, 1994).

46. Ibid., 960.

47. To learn more about the Paite *Inndongta*, see Kamkhenthang, *The Paite: A Transborder Tribe*, 15–86.

moving from one family's field to another's. All steps of cultivation, from burning the hill slopes in order to prepare the soil for the sowing of seeds, sowing of seeds, weeding and harvesting, were all done by both men and women.[48] All community members worked collectively and equally on all fields, led by a senior male leader (*lawm upa*), a boy attendant (*lawm naupang*), a female leader (*lawm nupi*) and a girl attendant (*lawmnu neu*).[49] The co-operative labor *Lawm* shows the harmonious communal nature of the tribe.

Each Paite village had a chief, *Hausa*, his appointed council of ministers, *Hausa Upate* ("chief's elders"), a village priest and a village crier. Generally, the chief was the one who planted and established a new village. There were also a few cases, however, where "the right to rule was with those who had the power and ability to command sufficient number of subjects, to be able to repel any attack from other chiefs."[50] As such, when disputes arose between two villagers, the physically stronger one would get the land and could establish himself as chief. Once established, by planting or by physical strength, village chieftainship is hereditary. Village chieftainship is retained and today each Paite village has a chief, albeit no longer holding sole leadership as there are now village authorities and local governments. Most Paite villages were established on hilltops rather than foothills, mainly for security and safety reasons, for ease of defense against surprise raids and attacks from other tribes or villages.

The Paite people are known to be humble, shy and peace-loving by nature, compassionate and generous to their co-villagers.[51] The Paite family basically consists of a father, a mother, and their children. Grandfathers, grandmothers, uncles, aunties, cousins, nieces and nephews and in-laws are often considered as being part of the same large family. The eldest son and his wife and their children are responsible for caring for the parents and all unmarried brothers and sisters. Accordingly, Paite families live together in the eldest son's house, which he usually inherited from his parents; the eldest son's house is called *innpi* (literally "main house").

Paite families have been patriarchal and patrilineal for time immemorial.[52] Belonging to a male-oriented and male-dominated society, Paite

48. Luai Chin Thang, "A History of the Evangelical Baptist Convention," 74–5.
49. Ibid., 76. *Upa* literally means "elder"; *naupang* means "child"; *nupi* means "woman" or "mother"; *nu* in *lawmnu neu* is the suffix for "female" and *neu* means "small" or "little."
50. *Hausa* literally means "rich." Liankhohau, *Social, Cultural, Economic and Religious Life*, 30.
51. Phaipi, "Mission Transformation for Evangelical Baptist Convention," 16.
52. Liankhohau, *Social, Cultural, Economic and Religious Life*, 22.

women are regarded as "subordinate and inferior to men in the estimation, concept and treatment of the male members."[53] Both the main governing institutions of the Paite tribe, the *Inndongta* at the household level and the customary laws at the tribe level, are also gender based. *Inndongta* excludes women from any speaking or decision-making roles, and the Paite customary laws in general serve male interests and preferences. The offices and positions of village chief, village elders, village priest and crier are exclusively male. The Paite are a spiritual people with their deep-rooted beliefs exhibited in their customs and traditions.

Paite Belief System
The Paite had a concept of God, whom they recognized as the creator, preserver, giver and the righteous one. This God they called *Pathian*, a masculine term (*pa* being the masculine signifier), or *Kouziin*, a neutral term that reflects the nature of being unseeable, strong and powerful at will, good and benevolent at will.[54] Religion was very much part of their everyday life experience. For example, when a dreadful storm occurred, a housewife would put a broom up on a hanging shelf over the cooking fireplace, called a *khin*, and exclaim *Pathian, zahngai in!*, meaning "God, be merciful!" Similarly, a poverty-stricken family, when in distress, would cry out, *Pathian thu thu hin teh*, meaning "It will be up to God." In addition to a belief in a supreme God, the Paites also believed in the existence of spirits in natural objects such as rocks, rivers, trees, streams and mountains, holding that these spirits have the ability to harm humans.[55] *Dawi*, devil or evil spirits, were believed to rule everywhere; as such, the Paites worshipped those natural objects in order to appease the wrath of the spirits. Essentially, the pre-Christian traditional worship of the Paites was animistic and fear-based.

Sacrifice was the principal means of worship. Chickens, birds, dogs and other animals were sacrificed to appease the spirits, typically in order to have sicknesses healed or so that the lands would be fertile. In conducting sacrifices, the priest, *siampi*, would chant *Tunga Pathian leh nuaia Pathian*, which means "the God above and the God below."[56] When conducting sacrifices to heal an ill person, a mud idol would be made and a priest would throw a spear at the spirit causing the illness and kill it. On such occasions, the great fear was that, in the event that the priest's

---

53. Phaipi, "Mission Transformation for Evangelical Baptist Convention," 18–19.
54. Liankhohau, *Social, Cultural, Economic and Religious Life*, 68.
55. Luai Chin Thang, "A History of the Evangelical Baptist Convention," 11.
56. Liankhohau, *Social, Cultural, Economic and Religious Life*, 69.

spear missed its target, the spirit would take possession of someone else (or even the priest); as such, no one dared to be nearby and anyone around remained in total silence.⁵⁷ The sacrificial system also indicates the important role played by the priest in the wider religious life of the Paite tribe, and by extension the successful functioning of the whole society. Without the priest, no sacrifice was possible, as he alone knew what type of sacrifice was needed for a particular illness or problem, and only he knew how the sacrifice was to be performed.⁵⁸ Such belief in and fear of spirits was the underlying concept in the religious life of the Paite. Upon conversion to Christianity, such beliefs would need to be accommodated into the Paite way of life.

One of the most prominent worship practices among the Paites was *Pisha*, which can also be associated with female deity worship since it began with the worship of a grandmother (*Pi* means "grandmother," and *sha* "worship").⁵⁹ According to the myth associated with this worship, an eagle dropped a snake on the paddy field of two orphaned brothers, Thanghou and Liandou. The snake then turned into an old woman who became grandmother to the boys. Whenever this grandmother shook her garments, millet grains fell out, which she would then cook for the brothers. The evening before her departure, she instructed the boys to offer a sacrifice of a white rooster with a spur whenever they felt apprehensive. The grandmother then sank down amidst the rice husks in the *sumtawng*, the porch-like corner of the house where the husking of rice is carried out. In memory of this instruction, Paite families performed *sumtawng* worship at least once a year in this area of their homes.⁶⁰

While all aspects of traditional worship and sacrificial practice were abolished following the Paite tribe's mass conversion to Christianity,⁶¹

---

57. Shinkhokam, *Pu-Pa Nun*, 103.
58. Luai Chin Thang, *A History of the Evangelical Baptist Convention*, 12.
59. Shinkhokam, *Pu-Pa Nun*, 90–4.
60. Luai Chin Thang, *A History of the Evangelical Baptist Convention*, 59.
61. Other forms of sacrificial worships practiced by the Paites, annually or throughout the year, include "Village Worship," *Nuhpi Kithoih, Gampi Kithoih, Loubawl, Lamkhak*, which may be briefly mentioned here. "Village Worship" was held at the beginning of each year for the welfare and prosperity of the entire village. *Nuhpi Kithoih* was performed to fight and heal sicknesses. Paites believed that sicknesses were caused by witchcraft and that in order to be healed the witchcraft had to be reversed. *Gampi Kithoih* was a form of sacrificial worship for the cure of sicknesses associated with the mind. *Loubawl* sacrifice was to ward off evil spirits living in deformed trees or banyan trees that were close to paddy fields or spring

many of these pre-Christian worship concepts would nevertheless be carried over into the tribe's Christian life. Let us now move on to an overview of the whole region of Northeast India.

Northeast India: A Brief Overview

"Northeast India" refers to the distinct region in the northeastern part of India, traditionally known as the "Seven Sisters," as it was comprised of the seven adjacent states of Assam, Arunachal Pradesh, Meghalaya, Manipur, Mizoram, Nagaland and Tripura. A new state, Sikkim, was added recently. Geographically, the region covers approximately 262,185 square kilometers of mostly difficult, mountainous terrain and river-intersected green valleys.[62] Northeast India shares its geographical borders with various political entities: Bangladesh to the west, Myanmar to the south and east, China (Tibet) to the northeast and Bhutan to the north. Northeast India is connected to the rest of India by a narrow corridor known as the "Chicken's Neck" which runs between Nepal to the north and Bangladesh to the south.

Referring to the whole region by a single term, "Northeast India," may give the impression that the region is a monochromatic entity, socially, culturally and politically. To a certain extent the region does indeed share some commonalities, and stands distinct from other parts of India, which is generally referred to as "mainland India." That is, from a geopolitical and ethnic standpoint, there is a certain commonality or even homogeneity which sees "all races…represented in a characteristic ethnic blend to be identified as Northeast Indian people."[63] Indeed, any casual visitor to Northeast India would recognize its inhabitants as different from mainland Indian people. Northeast India, however, is also certainly an amalgam of historically diverse ethnic groups with distinct languages and dialects, varied folklores, religions and mythologies. Nowhere in India are so many tribes concentrated as in the Northeast, and nowhere

---

water, as they were believed to cause sicknesses to the field owners. Finally, *Lamkhak*, which literally means "closing the way," is a preventative sacrificial practice against epidemics. For more details on the worship and offerings, see Luai Chin Thang, *A History of the Evangelical Baptist Convention*, 61–8.

62. http://databank.nedfi.com/content/general-information. Accessed on February 23, 2022.

63. Renthy Keitzar, "A Study of the North-East Indian Tribal Christian Theology," in *Society and Culture in North-East India: A Christian Perspective*, ed. Saral K. Chatterji (Delhi: Indian Society for Promoting Christian Knowledge, 1996), 118–19.

in the world is there a composition of population so diverse.[64] The ethnic composition of the Northeast region is rather a complex one.

Northeast India comprises three distinct groups of people, the hill tribes, the plain tribes and the non-tribal plains people, and each group is heterogenous. The hill tribes constitute local majorities within their territories, where their distinctive cultures have flourished in relative isolation.[65] The people making up the hill tribes display physical and cultural resemblances to Southeast Asians and are ethnologically similar to Tibetans and Mongoloids. It is widely agreed that the tribes of Northeast India are mainly from the Mongoloid heritage, with their ancestors having flocked into the region at a very early time. The generally accepted view is that Tibeto-Burmans from Indo-Chinese stock settled in the region from around 2000 BCE, migrating from the upper courses of the Yangtse-Kiang and the Hoang-Ho in northwest China.[66]

Politically, the Northeast indigenous communities were known to have not been under the rule of outside rulers. The tribes inhabited lands that had never belonged to anyone else or had never been under anyone else's custodianship.[67] The hill tribes were never a part of India and all the major villages had their own "village state" administration, managed according to their own customs and traditions, taboos and social systems that were quite different from those of the people of the valley.[68] Each hill village was self-governed, with three main stratifications: the village chief, the chief council members and the general populace of the village. The Northeast Indian tribes are known for their community life, communal ownership of their lands as well as the cooperative farming methods whereby all community members would work together and share in the harvest. Until the advent of the British Empire, most tribes in Northeast India lacked legal or political institutions transcending beyond the level of the individual village context.

The autonomy of the tribes of Northeast India came to an end with arrival of the British colonialists, who, in the form of the British East India Company, took control of the region from 1826. The colonialists

---

64. S. K. Khanna, *Encyclopaedia of North-East India: Arunachal Pradesh, Assam, Manipur, Meghalaya, Tripura, Sikkim, Mizoram, Nagaland* (Delhi: Indian Publishers' Distributors, 1999), 2.

65. Basumatary, *Ethnicity and Tribal Theology*, 39.

66. Ibid., 43.

67. Kaholi Zhimomi, "Northeast India," in *Christianity in South and Central Asia*, ed. Kenneth R. Ross, Daniel Jeyaraj, and Todd M. Johnson (Edinburgh: Edinburgh University Press, 2019), 157.

68. Basumatary, *Ethnicity and Tribal Theology*, 46.

established political control over Assam, Cachar, Manipur and Jaintia, which also resulted in the linking of the region politically with mainland India for the first time.[69] While the term "Northeast" functioned as an administrative, geographical category under British rule, it also made manifest distinctions based on racial underpinnings, and served to identify and differentiate the region and its occupants from mainstream India.[70] Such racialization and demarcation of the region persisted through the postcolonial times, with the annexation of the region into India.[71] In response to the reorganization or balkanization of the region into autonomous political units, the national integration policy-makers reconstituted the whole region into a single unit. Thus the Northeast Council (NEC) was formed in 1972 by order of the President of India. From then on, the term "Northeast India" has been liberally used by media, intelligentsia and bureaucracy alike as if these states were a single social and political entity, despite the fact that each state and each ethnic group had its own rich history, culture and religion.[72] All complexities considered, the true beauty of Northeast India remains in the fact that a uniquely warm bond ties together the age-old landscapes, histories, economies and cultures of the whole region. There is a oneness that transcends the political and imaginary boundaries that have been drawn and redrawn.

Religio-culturally, while the tribes of Northeast India did not have systematically organized social institutions or belief systems, they did have many common myths, beliefs, customs, rites and rituals. Most tribes had their own traditional religions, involving belief in a supreme being as well as other supernatural beings, such as spirits controlling life events. Over the course of history, the religious life of the tribes underwent major shifts, particularly with the arrival of the British. While a large number of

69. Zhimomi, "Northeast India," 156.

70. Imperial presence and power in this frontier region was established through the execution of various Acts, such as the Inner Line Regulation in 1873, the Frontiers Tracts Regulations of 1880 and the Schedules District Act of 1894, which were passed not just for economic reasons but "to separate the civilized plains people and the wild hill people." Jamir, "State, Patriarchy and Gender," 69–70.

71. In 1947, when India was on the verge of gaining independence from British imperial rule, the Northeast was basically ruled as Assam, minus Manipur and Tripura. But dismemberment of Assam began almost immediately. Sylhet, a predominantly Muslim area, was taken over by Bhutan, the Nagas demanded independence for Naga Hills, followed Mizo Hill tribes and others. By 1987, seven states were formed, each state having different processes. To read more about the formation of each state, see, for example, Khanna, *Encyclopaedia of North-East India*, 27–38.

72. Basumatary, *Ethnicity and Tribal Theology*, 34.

people in the plains of Assam, Manipur and Arunachal Pradesh accepted Hinduism (Brahmanical and Vaishnavism), which came from Northern India, tribes in the hills instead embraced the Christianity brought by missionaries who followed in the wake of British rule. Today, there is immense religious diversity in Northeast India, with Hindus, Muslims, Christians, Buddhists, Sikhs, Jains and practitioners of traditional religions all being found. While Hinduism predominates on the plains, Christianity is the principal religion of the hills. Three states with hill-tribe majorities, Meghalaya, Mizoram and Nagaland, can be considered majority Christian.

Conclusion

In this chapter we have looked at the general, pre-Christian-era situation of women as well as of the wider population of the region of Northeast India. The historical, socio-political and religio-cultural overview of the hill tribes of Northeast India has demonstrated that the tribes were autonomous, inhabiting self-governed villages that were established long ago. The tribes were also known to be closely interknitted communities, with self-sustained traditional economies and their own belief systems consisting of rites and rituals, worship and sacrifice. It can be easily seen that the tribes already had a deep-seated sense of spirituality even before Christianity was brought to them.

We have seen that pre-Christian customs and unscripted standards of tribal societies were subordinating to women. Yet we have also determined that the pre-Christian era was not without any trace of women's agency and that there were positions of prominence for women in certain areas. Just as a patriarchy does not of itself mean total absence of women's agency, so we have seen hints of the positive estimation of women within pre-Christian tribal societies such as the Paite. Considering that the pre-modern-period society was underdeveloped in general, when situated within their own times and standards, the pre-Christian situation of Paite women may not be too different from what we find today, with women still experiencing subordination within and outside the Church. This finding substantiates the relevance of the question whether the coming of missionaries and Christianity indeed brought with it an uplift for the status and condition of women. That question, as well as an exploration of the advent and impact of Christianity on Northeast India, will be taken up in the next chapter.

Chapter 2

Traditional Communities and Christianity

Introduction

In the previous chapter we learned that the hill tribes of Northeast India were self-governed, possessing their own village-specific systems of authority and self-sustaining economies. The tribes were also shown to be deeply religious, living in interknitted communities. Such was the context that greeted Western colonialists and Christian missionaries as they set foot on the Northeastern tribal lands, as they sought to bring about changes impacting on the lives of the tribal people. One of the changes Christianity brought was the elevated status of women, or so is often claimed. The question remains, however, whether the status of women has really been raised since, despite there being significant advancements in the professional lives of women—at times the advancements are greater than those enjoyed by men—the subordination of women remains systemic in tribal societies. As Lalmuoklien observes, parents themselves often remark that daughters/women "are just for sale like other commodities" and "this kind of treatment remained unchanged, in some cases, even after families became Christians."[1] He also notes how women were/still are treated as inferior beings, even after the coming of Christianity. More puzzling is the status of women in the Church, where they are consistently assigned subordinate roles—in spite of Christianity being credited with seeking to bring about the improvement of women's status. How can this paradox of the apparent elevation of women's status by Christian missionary movements and the sustained subordination of

---

1. Lalmuoklien, *Gospel Through Darkness: The History and the Missionary Work of the Northeast India General Mission (now ECCI) 1910–2004* (Churachandpur: Self-published, 2009), 10–11. ECCI stands for Evangelical Congregational Church of India.

women by Christianity and/or the Church be understood? To answer this question it is imperative to study the wider contexts. This is because any change, in this case the reinforcement of gender hierarchy, does not happen in isolation but is instead affected by other changes within the same or surrounding contexts.

In this chapter, we will survey briefly the coming of Christianity to Northeast India and the major changes brought to the tribes in the region by colonialism and Christianity. From our examination of the changes and the continuities from the pre-Christian, pre-colonial era, it will be shown that women's subordination continued not simply because the tribes remained patriarchal, but precisely because the missionary movements themselves were models of patriarchal structures/systems. It will also be observed that the ways the Bible is viewed and utilized in a tribal Christian society contribute to the subordination of women. That is, patriarchal tribes such as the Paite tribe found both a Christian and a biblical basis for gender subjugation in the form of the Christianity they embraced and their subsequent interpretation of Scripture. Before we begin a survey of the coming of Christianity, a preliminary pivotal question needs first to be addressed, namely, whether or not Christianity indeed brought changes to the tribal women's situation.

Women's Subordination and Christianity

Evaluating the status of women in a given community is complicated because, when viewed from the outside, women may appear to enjoy relative freedom. For instance, compared to rigid Hindu societies, Northeast Indian tribal women seem to have more freedom and are thus easily judged to enjoy higher status, one perhaps equal to men. However, when one understands the values controlling gender relations within that given society, it is not necessarily the case that women are held in high esteem. A more efficient methodology is to study the status of women in relation to that of the men in the same society, rather than making comparisons with other women in other societies.[2] The relevant question to ask, then, is whether or not the inner-tribal situation and perspective towards women changed or improved from what they were in pre-Christian times—without comparison to other tribes.

---

2. Frederick S. Downs, *The Christian Impact on the Status of Women in North East India: Professor H. K. Barpujari Endowment Lectures* (Shillong: North-Eastern Hill University Publications, 1996), 4.

What Ao calls "benevolent subordination" is very typical and true of Northeast Indian tribal women. She notes how particularly tribal men like to claim that their women are not subjugated because we do not practice outwardly visible subordinating practices such as dowry, *sati* and so on, customs practiced elsewhere in India. In reality, however, tribal women are allocated certain roles, ones strictly defined by their tribal "traditions," ones which say that "it is only men who can be decision-makers in important matters both in private and public affairs."[3] As Ao rightly states, women are subordinated within a benevolent-looking society, a socially constructed definition of the women so thorough that they themselves have accepted it as their ontological selfhood.[4] The subordination of women is sealed as the norm, natural and biblical, by citing selective biblical terms or verses; it is enforced through traditions and customs.

It is commonly assumed that Christianity brought progress to the tribal women of Northeast India, including members of the Paite. For example, writing eight decades after the coming of Christianity, Liankhohau claims that through the coming of Christianity women today enjoy a higher level of esteem then they had previously experienced. He claims that women are now "treated as equal to men," citing a biblical reference, Gal. 3:28: "For there is neither male nor female in Christ."[5] He notes some examples from the pre-Christian era to show the miserable situations that women had previously endured: how a husband took pride in divorce and marrying another; how wives were considered the property of their husbands; how a husband doing a domestic task for his wife would often be called *thai-nehlou*, "a henpecked husband," a derogatory label. Liankhohau does not, however, explain how the status of women really improved, except for mentioning that, after becoming Christians, the "husbands who help in household chores do not consider this below their dignity."[6] Such a statement is typical, but does not, in essence, imply any elevation of women's status. Rather, it is directed towards congratulating men for their modified outlook. That is, helping wives or women is supposedly below their dignity but, by not considering it so, the men demonstrate how magnanimous and generous they are.

---

3. Temsula Ao, "'Benevolent Subordination': Social Status of Naga Women," in *The Peripheral Centre: Voices from India's Northeast*, ed. Preeti Gill (New Delhi: Zubaan, 2010), 101.

4. Ibid., 105.

5. Liankhohau, *Social, Cultural, Economic and Religious Life*, 140.

6. Ibid.

The claim that Paite women are really treated as equal to men today can be refuted. The current Paite society is living evidence. As Liankhohau himself asserts, the same customs that served to subordinate women in the pre-Christian era are still practiced, even after the embracing of Christianity. Such conventions include the taking of a mate, the formation of the household council *inndongta*, as well as the bride price—as we saw in the previous chapter.[7]

In tribal societies, a married godly woman is expected to devote herself fully to her husband and his family, mainly through unconditional serving and submission; she is not to remain too closely connected with her *nolam* ("former" family). Such a standard is often interpreted and preached as the "Christian way," and one of the best ways to prevent family issues and problems because, it is said, unsubmissive and haughty women are the cause of family issues and problems. Most tribal Christian societies accept that it is a biblical proposition that women are subordinate to men. What Hangzo writes about Paite (Zomi) tribal women is an almost uncontested viewpoint: "Woman is considered as a helper to man, as 'Eve' was to 'Adam'," and a woman should model her behavior "according to Christian values as her spiritual life is one of the criteria for a good wife. But as for a man, the criteria cannot be decided by the woman. She has to accept him as he is if she loves him."[8] After more than a century of Christian influence in Northeast India, women continue to be excluded from any ministerial, pastoral or leadership positions, except within women-only groups, even though a large number of women have theological degrees. Women face comparatively more rigid restrictions within the Church than they experience in wider society in general.

If Christianity has not alleviated the situation of the tribal women, it is intriguing to ask why. Indeed, it seems likely that women's status was not changed at the foundational level in any meaningful way. In order to better understand the impact of Christian missionary movements on the status of women, it is first essential to understand the wider background of Christianity in Northeast India in the late nineteenth and early twentieth centuries. To analyze the impact of Christianity, we first need to survey briefly the coming of Christianity to Northeast India since this will provide broader awareness of the regional and historical contexts.

---

7. Ibid., 150–1.
8. Hangzo, "Gender Equality among the Zomis," 54–7.

The Coming of Christianity to Northeast India

The earliest presence of Christians in Northeast India dates back to the seventeenth and eighteenth centuries. The first known missionaries were Jesuits who worked in the Brahmaputra Valley in 1626.[9] Records also speak of the presence of two Roman Catholic churches in Lower Assam in 1696.[10] These early Christian missions apparently did not succeed in spreading Christianity, nor did the communities within which they worked seem to survive.

It was the advent of the British Empire in the first half of the nineteenth century that enabled several missions to work in Northeast India. The region became the focus of activity for six different missions during the nineteenth century: Serampore (British Baptist), American Baptist, Welsh Presbyterian, Roman Catholic, Anglican and Lutheran.[11] Although the Roman Catholics were the first known Christians to be present in Northeast India, the modern-era Catholic missionaries arrived much later than the Protestant ones. Modern Catholic missions in Northeast India began only from the year 1890, and the real growth of the Catholic Church in the entire Northeast India region happened only after the Independence of India (1947).[12] In a somewhat similar manner, while the Anglican clergy were the first to work in Assam with political and financial support as chaplains in the tea gardens and military camps since 1851, they showed little interest in evangelism to the native people.[13] A notable gift of the Anglican mission to the

---

9. Stephen Cacells and J. Gabral were the names of the Jesuits, and their real purpose was to explore a route into China and Tibet. F. S. Downs, "Early Christian Contacts with North East India," *ICHR* 5, no. 1 (1971): 70.

10. One of the Catholic churches was dedicated to Our Lady of the Rosary and the other to Our Lady of Guadelupe, at the Moghul garrison of Rangamati in Goalpara district of Lower Assam. These communities possibly came with the 63,000-strong Moghul army that Aurangazeb (in 1669) had sent against the Ahoms, and can perhaps be considered as the first fruits of the sixteenth- and seventeenth-century Jesuit missions to the Moghul. The communities disappeared soon after the Goalpara was ceded to the East India Company by the Moghuls in 1765, leaving no traces and without any discernible further spreading of Christianity. Downs, "Early Christian Contacts with North East India," 71.

11. Basumatary, *Ethnicity and Tribal Theology*, 66.

12. The coming of Fathers Otto Hopfenmueller and Angelus Muenzloher, Brothers Marianus Schumm and Joseph Bächle to Gauhati, Assam, on February 21, 1890 marked the beginning of the modern Catholic mission. Ibid., 69.

13. Consequently, by the end of the nineteenth century, there were barely 500 local Anglicans. Ibid., 70.

community was their translation of the New Testament into the Kachari language. The Lutheran mission also faced a comparable fate when the Lutheran mission in Assam, which started in 1860, came to an end after the founder left the mission.[14] Among the different denominations and mission agencies, the Baptists (British Baptist Mission and then American Baptist Mission) and the Welsh Presbyterian Mission (earlier Welsh Calvinistic Methodist) were the most impactful ones. It is no surprise that the Christianity of Northeast India displays general similarities with traditional Baptist and Presbyterianism in the West, such as in doctrinal beliefs and administrative structuring.

The first significant missionary contact with Northeast India was made by the Serampore mission of the British Baptist Missionary Society in the early part of the nineteenth century. Interestingly, the initiative came from British government officials because the government officials were unsuccessful in their military expedition owing to endless wars or retaliation and revenge from the tribals.[15] Thus Christian missionaries were utilized by the British imperialists as a "mission of civilization," a means to tame the "unruly," and "humanize" the wild tribes of the Northeast Frontier.[16] The invitation to engage with the tribal communities was received warmly by the missionaries, as they were able to utilize the British government's resources in their mission work, particularly for education and security. Colonialism and mission movements thus had mutual benefits and the impacts they made also overlap in several ways.

Bringing about change among the tribal people, so that they aligned to the imperialist agenda, seemed to be the primary motive behind the colonialists' interest in mission. When the judge of Sylhet in Khasi hills, W. N. Garrett, invited the Baptist missionary William Carey in 1813 to evangelize the Khasis, he even suggested that the tribal members be baptized and made Christians outright, with doctrinal teachings

---

14. The Lutheran mission was started at Tezpur, Assam by the missionary Hesselmeyer. After the founder left the mission, many of the Adivasi tea-garden workers who were Lutherans went back to their traditional faiths while others joined other churches, such as Baptists and Anglicans. At the close of the nineteenth century, there were two functioning Lutheran Churches in Assam, the Gossner Evangelical Lutheran Church (GELC) and Northern Evangelical Lutheran Church (NELC). Today, there are around 500 Lutheran congregations in Northeast India. Ibid., 70–1.

15. Lal Dena, *Christian Missions and Colonialism: A Study of Missionary Movement in Northeast India with Particular Reference to Manipur and Lushai Hills 1894–1947* (Shillong: Vendrame Institute, 1988), 18–19.

16. Ibid., 20.

following later.[17] William Carey readily accepted the terms, most likely because he had already begun translating the Bible into Khasi. He duly sent a local convert, Krishna Chandra Pal, to work among the Khasis. But against the high expectation of the government, only two Khasis and five Assam natives were baptized after eight months of outreach. Though the Serampore mission had little impact on the people, the mission made significant contributions, with its translation of the New Testament into Assamese (1819), Khasi (1824) and Manipuri (1827).[18] Needless to say, these translated Bibles would become the core resources and assets for the tribal Christians later, and directly or indirectly would play a substantial role in imparting and transmitting concepts such as gender opinions. In 1833 the Serampore mission sent more missionary teams who, in addition to evangelizing, would work to establish three schools in three different locations.[19] Evangelism, Bible translations and education went hand-in-hand, which would be the trend in missionary work that followed too.

After some years, the Serampore Mission dropped both the Khasi and Assam fields owing to financial constraints and a lack of workers. The American Baptist mission took over the lower Assam region while the Welsh Calvinistic Methodist Mission stepped into the Khasi field. From March 1836, the American Baptists then started working among the Khamti and Singpho tribes at the upper extremity of the Brahmaputra Valley.[20] By December of 1845 a Baptist church was established and two branches organized in the same year in Nagaon and Sibsagar, marking their beginnings of mission in the Northeast region. The Khasi hills mission was taken up by the Welsh Calvinistic Methodists (known

---

17. The Khasis were apparently refugees from the neighboring inter-tribal wars who had taken up residence in the territory belonging to the East India Company. Downs, "Early Christian Contacts with North East India," 71; Basumatary, *Ethnicity and Tribal Theology*, 66–7.

18. Basumatary, *Ethnicity and Tribal Theology*, 67.

19. The American Baptist Mission working in Assam after the British Baptist Mission was mainly motivated by their perception of the region as a gateway to their primary goal of opening a mission in China and northern Burma. The missionaries were the Anglo-Indian pair, Alexander B. Lish and Joshua Roe. They came to Cherrapunji, located just above Sylhet. They founded schools in 1838. Downs, "Early Christian Contacts with North East India," 72.

20. The first missionaries were the families of Nathan Brown and Oliver Cutter, and their first Assamese convert, Nidhiram, was baptized on June 13, 1841. Downs, "Early Christian Contacts with North East India," 75; Basumatary, *Ethnicity and Tribal Theology*, 67–8.

as Welsh Presbyterians from the early twentieth century).[21] Thomas Jones from Montgomeryshire arrived in the region on June 22, 1841 and established a mission station at Cherrapunji. The Welsh mission gradually expanded beyond the Khasi hills, taking in the Lushai hills that later extended to the south Manipur tribes such as the Paites. Let us now take a look at the arrival of Christianity to the state of Manipur, the main state where most Paites lived.

The Coming of Christianity to Manipur
Our survey of the historical background to the missionary activity will now continue with a brief general presentation of the state of Manipur.[22] Manipur is a small state in Northeast India, bounded by Myanmar to the east, Nagaland to the north, Assam to the west and Mizoram to the south. Geographically, the state covers around 22,000 square kilometers of mostly hilly terrain; only about 1680 square kilometers of the Manipur state are valley.[23] The valley lands occupy a central position within the state, and it is here that the capital, Imphal, is located. Imphal is the hub of all political and social institutions. The central valley is surrounded by hills on all sides. Essentially, the state of Manipur is divided into two main tracts—the hills, which are mainly inhabited by the tribes, and the valley plains, which are mainly inhabited by Meitei plains people. Politically, the kingdom of Manipur remained outside of India until its annexation by the British following the 1891 Anglo-Manipur War. The hill tribes had up until this time been autonomous communities inhabiting their own self-governed villages. In 1949 Manipur was made part of the Indian Union, and became a full-fledged Indian state in 1972.

---

21. The Welsh Calvinistic Methodist Foreign Mission Society was formed in 1840, but originally operated through the London Missionary Society (1795), which was a conglomeration of Anglicans, Welsh Presbyterians and Congregationalists/Independents who broke away from the Society because of sectarian feelings within the Society. Issues that resulted in the break-up included conflicting opinions on Church polity and policies on missionary recruitment, which rejected candidates from Presbyterians on mere grounds of their being Methodists. Dena, *Christian Missions and Colonialism*, 26. To read more about the London Mission Society and the formation of the Calvinistic Methodists' Foreign Mission Society, see John Hughes Morris, *The History of the Welsh Calvinistic Methodists' Foreign Mission, to the End of the Year 1904* (Carnarvon: C. M. Book Room, 1910), 1–37.

22. For a fuller discussion of the historical situation of Manipur, see Karam Manmohan Singh, *History of the Christian Missions in Manipur and Neighbouring States* (New Delhi: Mittal Publications, 1991), 1–33.

23. Khanna, *Encyclopaedia of North-East India*, 355.

Missionaries who wished to travel to Manipur in the nineteenth century had to clear three layers of administrative structures—the Manipur State Durbar, the Political Agent and the Maharaja. A prior permission of the Durbar through the Political Agent had to be obtained. Up until 1891, "the relation between Manipur and British India was limited to the recognition and regulation of each successive king and the stationing of a British officer with the objective of guiding the ruling maharaja."[24] In addition, Vaishnavite Hinduism had already been made a principal state religion by means of royal edict in 1705, meaning that movements of white people were looked upon with suspicion.[25] In such a religio-political situation the early attempts of the American Baptist Mission to establish its mission station in Manipur as early as 1839 proved futile. The Welsh Mission had also sought to establish a mission field in Manipur, without success. When Manipur suffered defeat in the Anglo-Manipur war of 1891, however, Christian mission lines opened up.

The first missionary to work in Manipur was William Pettigrew, from the Arthington Aboriginese Mission Society. He arrived in Imphal on February 6, 1894 with the full patronage of the Political Agent of Manipur.[26] However, the Meiteis, plains people of Manipur who were conservative Hindus, rejected Pettigrew's preaching as they viewed it as an attempt to impose the "government's religion." The British government also had a social policy of "non-interference" or "strict neutrality" of British India within princely states. Therefore, Maxwell, the Political Agent of Manipur, was compelled to ask Pettigrew to stop his missionary activity on the plains and suggested the possibility of working in the hill areas instead.[27] Upon learning of the circumstances on the ground, Pettigrew's sponsoring agency, the Arthington Mission, ceased sponsoring him, leaving him with no option but to apply for membership of the American Baptist Missionary Union in Assam. The Baptist Missionary Conference at Sibsagar in 1895 subsequently designated Pettigrew as a missionary to Manipur subject to his ordination by the Sibsagar Baptist

24. Dena, *Christian Missions and Colonialism*, 31.
25. Ibid.
26. The Arthington Aboriginese Mission Society was named after Robert Arthington, a millionaire from Leeds, northern England. The same Mission also sent two missionaries, J. H. Lorrain and F. W. Savidge, to Lushai hills, south of Manipur. Ibid., 32.
27. This was enacted after the revolt of 1857, particularly in matters of religion. Any departure from such policy would very likely be seized upon by the Hindus in Bengal and elsewhere as grounds for an attack upon the government. It would also be construed as a breach of so-called neutrality. Ibid., 34.

Church, Assam.[28] Accordingly, the Baptists began their mission work in the northern Manipur hill country of Ukhrul with Pettigrew as its missionary.

Not much evangelistic work was achieved in the opening years of the mission as Pettigrew was engaged with building a mission bungalow, teaching, studying the local dialect and doing translation work, handing out medicines and assisting the state officials. Pettigrew repeatedly petitioned for another missionary to assist him, and eventually the American Baptist Mission Union assigned another missionary, U. M. Fox, to Ukhrul in 1911. Socialized in a largely secular American society, Fox's concept of missionization was not determined solely by religious factors. Thus, besides itinerary evangelism, Fox also trained the native people in practical skills such as carpentry and metalwork, thereby enabling them to make modern furniture and also build mission centers.[29] As such, the missionary efforts can be said to have fostered material comfort and improvements in lifestyle among the tribal people. Gradually, this mission in the northern Manipur hills expanded to the western part, the Sadar hills.[30] The hill areas on the southern part of Manipur were also to encounter Christianity, albeit from another mission.

The Coming of Christianity to the Paite Tribe in South Manipur

Although Manipur was claimed to be the mission field of the American Baptist Mission, the whole of Manipur had not yet been reached. The untrodden southern Manipur hills encountered the Christian Gospel for the first time in 1910, through the efforts of an independent worker who had been accompanying the Welsh Mission. The Lushai hills became part of the British Empire in 1891, paving the way for the entry of missionaries. William Williams, a Welsh missionary working in the Khasi hills, came to the Lushai hills on March 20, 1891 and, after making a positive assessment, appealed to the Liverpool home board. Concurrently getting the agreement of the British officials in Assam, the Lushai hills became part of the Welsh mission field in June 1892.

---

28. The American Baptist Mission judged that he did not hold views contrary to their "distinctive doctrines," most probably the believer's baptism, and accepted him to be their missionary.

29. Dena, *Christian Missions and Colonialism*, 37.

30. The increased number of local churches and the widening of the frontier of missionary movement also necessitated the formation of the very first Christian association in Manipur, known as the Manipur Christian Association, in November of 1916, which held its first convention in 1917 in Ukhrul. Ibid., 38.

The first missionary to bring Christianity to southern Manipur hill tribes, including the Paite, was Watkin R. Roberts, who accompanied the missionary doctor Dr. Peter Fraser and his wife Mary C. Fraser to Lushai hills in December of 1908.[31] Upon learning from one of their clinic patients, from Senvon village in Churachandpur district of south Manipur, that he and his fellow villagers had never heard of Christianity and also that their chief could read Lushai, Roberts immediately sent a copy of the Gospel of John in Lushai (Mizo) to their chief.[32] Not understanding the book, the village chief sent it back, along with the message, "Sir, come yourself, and tell us about this book and your God." The chief also allowed a mission station to be established on his land.[33] Roberts duly sought the government's permission to cross the border, recruited two natives, Lungpau Vaiphei and Thangkhai Vaiphei, who were studying at Aizawl under the sponsorship of Dr. Fraser, and set out for Senvon.[34] The three men arrived in Senvon on February 5, 1910 after a week of walking through several villages, crossing rivers and deep forests. After preaching the gospel in Senvon and other neighboring villages for about a month, they returned to Aizawl. Roberts then recruited three new converts, Savawma, Vanzika and Thangchhingpuia, to go and continue the mission work in southern Manipur. The following year, 1911, another native convert from Mizoram, Taisena, joined as an evangelist at Senvon, and so the mission in the south Manipur district of Churachandpur continued to grow.

Meanwhile, Roberts' pioneering mission work in southern Manipur came to be seen as a breach of the comity of Protestant Mission Societies in India, as he had not informed the American Baptist Mission, who

31. Watkin R. Roberts was a chemist, who undertook missioning work during the Welsh Revival of 1904–6 and the Keswick Convention of 1907. Dr. Peter Fraser (1864–1919) and his wife Mary C. Fraser were the first medical missionaries sent by the Welsh Calvinistic Foreign Mission Society; they arrived in Aizawl, the capital of Mizoram, on October 14, 1908. Phaipi, "Mission Transformation for Evangelical Baptist Convention, India," 24.

32. Watkin Roberts (1886–1969) had received a gift of £5 Sterling from Emily Davies of north Wales, which he used to purchase 104 copies of the Gospel of John that had been translated into Lushai (Mizo) language by missionaries J. H. Lorrain and F. W. Savidge. Roberts distributed these copies of the Gospel of John to village chiefs in Mizoram and the surrounding region, along with letters explaining the way to salvation through Christ. Ibid., 25.

33. Dena, *Christian Missions and Colonialism*, 49.

34. Khupkhothang, *Chanchinpha Vak Hun Pawlut Masate* [Those Who First Brought the Good News Light] (Churachandpur: Evangelical Organization Church, 1992), 8–9. Cited by Phaipi, "Mission Transformation for Evangelical Baptist Convention," 26.

already viewed Manipur as their mission field, of his activities.³⁵ The Welsh Mission then cautiously made a statement that Roberts was not considered a regular missionary; he was not officially recognized by their mission society nor by any other. Under these circumstances, even though Roberts was warmly welcomed by the native people, he never had the opportunity to live among them because of government restrictions. The mission station he founded had to be run mostly by native workers.³⁶ At the same time, the Welsh Mission could not fully disown Roberts and his mission in southern Manipur as the first of Roberts' converts were engaged in the running of the new missionary outpost. So, in December 1913, R. Dala was sent out as a first native missionary from Lushai hills to be the field superintendent of the pioneer mission. Along with the assistance of teacher-evangelists Savawma, Vanzika and Taisena, the mission work grew and within a short time the mission spread to over twenty villages. A primary school was opened, enabling local people to read the Bible. The next year, on December 10, 1914, the first presbytery was convened at Senvon, with R. Dala as Chairman and Taisena as Secretary. Therefore, the first native missionaries to the southern Manipur district of Churachandpur, where the Paite tribe is a majority, were Mizos from Lushai hills (Mizoram). The first hymnals and Bibles used were in Mizo languages, which were gradually reproduced into Paite.

In sum, the mission work undertaken in Northeast India opened up in the late nineteenth and early twentieth centuries following the arrival of British imperialism. The missions were successful particularly in the hills and saw hill tribes convert en masse to Christianity. Slowly, mission works were turned over to indigenous Christian bodies. The Welsh Presbyterians handed over their mission work to indigenous churches in 1941, with the American Baptists doing the same in 1950.³⁷ Today, Christianity is the primary religion among the hill tribes and the major religion in the states of Meghalaya, Mizoram and Nagaland. The large and heavily populated

35. The policy of the Protestant Mission Societies in India required a new missionary or mission agency not to undertake any work without a prior understanding from the mission already there. In August of 1911 William Pettigrew made inquiries such as whether Roberts, Dr. Fraser or the Welsh Mission intended to take up work in Manipur. The Welsh Mission District committee then had to make inquiries regarding Roberts' motivation for undertaking the new mission work. Further details on the conflicts between Roberts and Pettigrew, including proposals for co-operation between the two, are documented by several people, including Singh, *History of the Christian Missions*, 180–260.
36. Dena, *Christian Missions and Colonialism*, 50–1.
37. Downs, "Christian Conversion Movements in North East India," 396.

states of Assam, Manipur and Tripura remain predominantly Hindu, and Sikkim continues to be a Buddhist majority state. In the case of Manipur, almost all the hill areas are majority Christian.[38] The proliferation of the new Christian religion brought to the Northeast India hill areas was surely to have immense impact on the people, to which we now turn.

Impacts of Christianity on Northeast Indian Tribes

In analyzing the impacts of Christianity within Northeast Indian tribal communities, the broader consequences of British colonialism cannot be ignored. For indeed, not only was British rule responsible for enabling entry of Christian missions into Northeast India, but also the changes it brought about became intertwined with those of the Christian missionary movements. And although our main interest is on how Christianity affected gender relations in tribal societies such as the Paite's, it must be accepted that any impact in one area of society could not have happened in isolation. As such, it is imperative to consider the general and wide-ranging impacts the tribal societies encountered from the intrusion of British imperialists and the coming of the missionaries. There is also the question of whether it was indeed Christianity, or rather British imperialism, that imposed the changes in the first place. So, this latter issue will briefly be addressed first.

Some attribute the socio-cultural changes to British imperialism. For example, Downs argues that it was the British rule that imposed rapid and sometimes tragic changes on the region of Northeast India, and in that circumstance Christianity served as a guardian to preserve tribal identities and traditions.[39] On the other hand, others, like Zhimomi, contend that the missionaries themselves were responsible for any negative impacts on the tribal peoples. She argues that the missionaries devalued and discriminated the tribal spirituality and culture, and "instead of reforming indigenous customs, missionaries tried to replace them comprehensively

---

38. The census of the main religions in Manipur per 10,000 of the whole population showed growth in the number of Christians, from 45 in 1901 to 132 in 1911 (Hindus were 5996 in 1901 and 5816 in 1911; Animists were 3631 in 1901 and 3735 in 1911). Singh, *History of the Christian Missions*, 32.

39. Downs elaborated his claims in a few places, including "Christianity as a Tribal Response," 408–16, "Faith and Life-style: How Christianity was Understood by Nineteenth Century Converts in North East India," *Bangalore Theological Forum* 14, no. 1 (January–June 1982): 20–43, and "Christianity and Socio-Cultural Change in the Hill Areas of North East India," *ICHR* 26, no. 1 (1992): 50–62.

with Western manners, customs and spirituality."[40] This led to the colonized and Christianized tribes developing pessimistic attitudes towards their own religions and culture, eventually regarding and adopting Western culture and religion as "superior."

Considering the nature of the changes, my view is that the Christian missionaries and the British rulers share responsibility for impacting the changes in Northeast India. It is my view that while "secular" elements of life, such as the economic and political systems, were directly and self-evidently impacted by British rule, the Christian mission agencies had deeper and perhaps more subtle influences that touched on the religious life and morality of the tribal people, including changes in the style of dress, prohibition of rice-beer and the like. At the same time, the changes cannot be totally separated from one another since all areas of tribal life are interknitted, with changes in one area having a clear effect on neighboring areas. When it comes to the subordination of women, colonialism and Christianity both seem to have provided the models and structures that created and sustained it. Neither system appears to have brought radical, positive change at the foundational, ideological level. That is, while women seem to enjoy better living conditions than they had previously experienced—something that is actually true for men and women alike—in the wider society the notion of women as subordinate remained.

While the imperial government obviously had far-reaching impacts on the tribal communities, the Christian missionaries were the ones who shared in the daily lives, the significant and mundane moments, of the native people. Consequently, over and above what they taught directly through evangelism, as well as in school and Church settings, the ways the missionaries acted and structured their daily lives also had an influence. The missionary habits were readily perceived as "the Christian way" and subsequently adopted by the newly converted tribals. In that sense, the missionaries were influential agents of change—and lack of change—be that intentionally and unintentionally. Downs, who attributes most changes to British imperialism, was forced to admit that while British imperialism was the primary cause of the changes, Christianity, which was acculturative, in due course became causative in relation to socio-cultural developments.[41] In fact, the missionaries were committed to change whatever they deemed "unchristian" in the customs and cultures

---

40. Zhimomi, "Northeast India," 159–60.

41. "Causative" means the primary cause of change, while "acculturative" means "being an instrument through which people are helped to adjust to changes that are already irreversibly being thrust upon them by other agencies." Downs, "Christianity and Socio-Cultural Change," 54.

of the tribes. And in so doing, the missionaries also became cohesive agents of imparting their own ideologies, moral and cultural standards as if they were the Christian and biblical ways. That is to say, the Christian missionary movements should be viewed as responsible and, if necessary, culpable for bringing about change and lack of change within the converted tribal societies.

We shall now briefly summarize some of the major changes Northeast India went through with the coming of colonialism and Christianity.

Loss of Autonomy
One major change that the tribes of Northeast India underwent was the loss of their autonomy. These tribes—who had been living in villages they founded by clearing the hilly areas and making them inhabitable, governing with their own village-state administration—were subjected to external political authority, the British. Through their "indirect rule," the British political authorities recognized and used the village chief as the linchpin for ruling their subjects.[42] This sudden shift of governance would have been traumatic and served to dramatically change the way of relating within their interknitted communities. The arrival of the British colonial powers most certainly caused intra- and inter-village harmony to crumble.

New Economy: Money
Another notable impact was the introduction of the money-based economy in tribal societies. The pre-colonial tribal economy was a traditional economy based on community life where the land was communally owned, the labor co-operative and the harvest shared.[43] Along with the money economy also came "consumer goods such as mill cloth and kerosene lanterns which undermined the largely self-sufficient economies of the tribes and created new concepts of wealth."[44] The pursuit of personal wealth became pervasive, as did the ideas of profit, individual gain and success. The new economy based on money gradually widened the gender gap as men came to be seen as the money earners, with women being confined to roles of homemakers and childrearers. The valuable contributions of women were monetarily unmeasurable.

---

42. Dena, *Christian Missions and Colonialism*, 42.

43. This is a widely acknowledged practice among different tribes, one that often goes undisputed by many. See, for example, T. T. Cooper, *New Routes for Commerce: The Mishmee Hills* (1873), 149, cited in Verrier Elwin, ed., *India's North-East Frontier in the Nineteenth Century* (Bombay: Oxford University Press, 1959), 370.

44. Downs, "Christianity as a Tribal Response," 408.

The colonial market economy also produced a new land administration system that created a new, all-male landlord class. This further empowered males and thereby created an unhealthy gender imbalance.[45] Furthermore, with the commercialization of agriculture, men began to have more say in cropping decisions and money matters while women's voices remained unheard—even though it was the women who were typically toiling for endless hours in the fields.[46] Women's value and status became diminished, or so it was perceived, while men gained status and power through the new instruments and structure in the money economy.

Education

Education and schools were the combined effort of the British imperialists and missionaries. For the missionaries, the Bible was the ultimate source of authority, such that all of Christian life and worship should abide by biblical teachings; therefore, it was imperative that the converts were able to read the Bible.[47] For the colonial officials, their interest in the mission's educational programs was more imperialistic than paternalistic. For them, the education imparted by the missionaries was effective in both "taming" and "civilizing" the natives and thereby enabling them to be loyal subjects.[48] Consequently, it can be said that the education of tribal communities served symbiotic purposes, with the missionaries running the schools and the British government providing the funding.

In education, however, there was a marked prejudice towards the education of girls. "The education imparted must be such as to make the girls an asset in their community."[49] The idea of girls as "assets" is particularly important here and indicates how a girl's manual contribution at home and within the community came to be estimated. Accordingly, trained lady missionaries formulated curricula whereby the girls' learning would be both educational as well as potentially financially profitable.[50] Such issues were absent for the boys' schooling. In essence, then, while education was indeed a positive change for the tribals, it appears that

---

45. This is through new colonial market instruments like Agreements and Settlements. Ray, "Tribal Women in North-East India," 48.
46. Ibid., 52.
47. Dena, *Christian Missions and Colonialism*, 90.
48. Ibid., 90–1.
49. Ibid., 97.
50. The practical work for girls includes weaving, needlecraft, basket-making, clay pottery, childcare, knitting and crochet, gardening, farm labor (including breeding of cattle and poultry), household management, singing, dancing, and so on. Ibid., 98.

schools also fundamentally functioned as gender segregators. More on this below.

Change in Lifestyle

One of the most notable impacts of the Christian missionaries is that they ushered in peaceful relationships among the former head-hunting Northeast Indian tribes.[51] The British government brought a direct end to inter-tribal raids by means of external force. At the same time, however, the missionaries, preaching the biblical message of love for neighbors and enemies, provided the ideological basis for peaceful interaction between different tribes. Young men of the warrior age who converted would become involved in evangelism to neighboring tribes who had traditionally been their enemies.[52]

The missionaries also enforced change of lifestyle at the individual level. The missionaries considered changing the lifestyles of the converts to be an end goal, as can be seen in the mission statement of the region's pioneer evangelist movement, the Welsh mission. It states that for church membership, a "candidate should not only have renounced all heathen practices and lead a moral life," but also that he must "possess an intelligent knowledge of Christian principles, observe the Sabbath, and abstain from all intoxicants."[53] In order to be considered a good-standing Christian, converts were expected to live by accepted standards, involving abstention from the use of intoxicants (drinking alcohol, smoking tobacco), adoption of hygienic living conditions, advocacy of a more prominent and dignified role for women, opposition to intra-tribal warfare and head-hunting, and the use of traditional institutions such as bachelor dormitories.[54] On the one hand, a change in lifestyle might be seen as a clear, outward sign of the acceptance and adoption of a new religion. On the other hand, it is difficult to be certain that a change of lifestyle necessarily involved a doctrinally or theologically based change of ideology, or whether changes in behavior were (merely) superficial displays of a desire to conform. A consideration of one change common to most tribes, denunciation of rice-beer, will be helpful here.

51. Downs, "Faith and Life-style," 27.
52. The Assamese were the first evangelists among the Ao and Angami Nagas, who in turn evangelized among other neighboring tribes. The Nagas in Manipur were involved in early evangelization of the Kukis. A Khasi convert was involved in the founding of the Church in Mizoram, and the Mizos were involved in the evangelism of southern Manipur and so on.
53. Morris, *The History of the Welsh Calvinistic Methodists' Foreign Mission*, 91.
54. Downs, "Faith and Life-style," 23.

It is curious to consider what drove the missionaries' prohibition of rice-beer, which is generally seen in tribal Christian societies as incompatible with Christianity. With the coming of the missionaries, writes Kamkhenthang, "Drinking of rice-beer, ritual offering of rice-beer to Kinsmen [sic] and evil spirit are set aside only for the non-Christians and not for the new converts. Rice-beer, which was ubiquitous in every household, lost its ritual value. Religious values enforced by rice-beer can no longer be sustained without rice-beer."[55] Having once being associated with tribal religion, the consumption of rice-beer (and alcohol more generally) became singularly incompatible with the new religion. Indeed, the negative attitude towards drinking among the Paite Christians persists even today—drinking alcohol is considered a sin, and drinking alcohol and being Christian are considered mutually exclusive. And yet, interestingly, the missionaries' opposition to the use of intoxicants such as opium and alcohol was not so much driven from a theological stance, but rather stemmed from their background of having seen the problem of alcoholism in urban centers created by the Industrial Revolution in Britain and the United States.[56] We might say that the social experiences of the missionaries became entwined with the theological message they delivered and the personal lives they lived. My point here is certainly not to commend drinking or a drinking lifestyle. Instead, I mention this only as an example of how the stringent prohibition of drinking, as though biblically or theologically endorsed, derived from the missionaries' own ideologies and standards. A comparable understanding of gender subjugation can be observed, as will be discussed below.

Creation of Literature

One of the most significant contributions of the missionaries was the preservation of the native tribal languages and the creation of literature

55. H. Kamkhenthang, "Christianity *vis-à-vis* Tribal Religion in Manipur," in *Religion in Northeast India*, ed. Soumen Sen (New Delhi: Uppal Publishing House, 1993), 43.

56. The Protestant missionaries who came to Northeast India were from countries that had temperance movements opposed to consumption of alcoholic beverages, while the Catholic missionaries were from Continental Europe, which did not oppose the consumption of alcohol in moderation. The varying views on alcohol became the cause of conflict among the missionaries and, in fact, this issue remains one of the main distinguishing features of the two churches today. Frederick S. Downs, *History of Christianity in India, Volume 5, Part 5: Northeast India in the Nineteenth and Twentieth Centuries* (Bangalore: The Church History Association of India, 1992), 147.

for tribes who might otherwise have been made to adopt Bengali or some other common language by the British government.[57] All or most of the tribes of Northeast India have a myth or legend about how they lost their scripts owing to some accident or carelessness. Such myths might involve a man losing the script while swimming in a river, dropping it in a fire or a hole, or by placing it somewhere that allowed it to be eaten by animals.[58] In the case of the Paite tribe, legend has it that the only copy of their script, written on animal skin, was eaten by a dog and thus unrecoverable.[59] In such scenarios, the missionaries utilized the Roman letters to help in the formulation of alphabets.

The first Paite primer, *Paite Bubul*, was created in 1903 on the initiative of the missionary David E. Jones and his assistant T. Vialphung, a Paite and mission school student.[60] The alphabet was modified in 1945 by Rev. H. Nengzachin, one of the first Paite Christian leaders, and this system continues to be used today for writing the Paite language.[61] The missionaries' efforts to create a script for the Paite tribe paved the way for the translation and development of the Paite Bible and other documents such as hymnals. Importantly, the development of literacy and written

57. Basumatary, *Ethnicity and Tribal Theology*, 76.

58. Downs even describes these stories as resembling, in their mythological function, the garden of Eden/Fall story of the Judeo-Christian tradition. Downs, "Christianity and Socio-Cultural Change," 61.

59. Apparently, they used objects and signs for communication; for example, the sending of a stick tied to a parcel of red peppers to a village represented a declaration of war or intended enemy attack. Liankhohau, *Social, Cultural, Economic and Religious Life*, 110.

60. David E. Jones came to Aizawl in the Lushai Hills in 1897. Liankฅ hohau, *Social, Cultural, Economic and Religious Life*, 120; H. Thangtungnung and S. Ngulzadal, *History of Paite Literature*, https://www.academia.edu/34934290/HISTORY_OF_PAITE_LITERATURE. Accessed on February 10, 2022.

61. A year after the Paite Primer was created, the Paite language was listed in Grierson's linguistic survey of Northeast India. George Abraham Grierson, *Languages of North-Eastern India, Volume 2* (New Delhi: Gyan Publishing House, 1995), 574.

Nengzachin dropped the letters Q, W, X and Y, and combined A and W as AW to form long the O sound. The Paite alphabet consists of twenty-four letters: A AW B CH D E F G NG H I J K L M N O P R S T U V Z. Worship songs in Paite were also published, actually before the Paite Bible translations appeared. The first hymnal for the church was printed in 1942. In 1969, *Pathian Ngaih La*, a song book of devotional or spiritual songs was published, and in 1970 the Church published a hymn book, *Biakna Late*, with tonic solfa notations. *Pathian Ngaih La* contains songs with tunes that closely relate to the traditional melodies of the Paite tribal music, while *Biakna Late* are hymns mostly translated from English.

culture did not stop there. What began as an elementary school education with the primary aim of enabling Bible reading, has continued and resulted in the preservation and composition of native tribal literature. This, undoubtedly, has been a true gift from missionaries to the tribes of Northeast India.[62]

In sum, Christianity and colonialism brought many profound and visible changes to Northeast India, among the hill tribes in particular. Some changes, such as loss of autonomy, adversely affected the overall nature of the tribes and the communal relationships between them. Other changes, such as education and the money economy, reinforced the male–female gender gap. Still others, such as the prohibition of rice-beer, have influenced the nature of the understanding of the tribes' new religion. Notwithstanding these extensive changes, there are also continuities, particularly at the deep ideological level.

Continuities Between Pre-Christianity and the Advent of Christianity

Pre-Christian ideologies found their way into Christian dogma, sometimes in new forms and other times in virtually the same forms with new bases in Christian teachings. First and foremost, there is much continuity between earlier perspectives of God/Supreme Being. The Christian God proved to be attractive to the native people primarily based on their observation that this God is more powerful than the other god(s) they worshipped, and because he could be relied upon to save them from tragedy and difficulties. Missionaries reported that they found a point of contact with the tribals when they proclaimed Jesus as the strong divine victor, the vanquisher of the Devil.[63] The concept of God as the savior from difficulties was retained. Religion based on fear continued.

The tribal belief in the existence of evil spirits controlling daily life events, and with that the fear of such spirits, persisted even after the

---

62. Altogether, throughout the Northeast, Christian missionaries were responsible for developing a written form of at least fifty different languages. Downs, "Christian Conversion Movements in North East India," 389.

63. This is according to a missionary report made by J. Herbert Lorrain and F. W. Savidge, cited by Thanzauva and R. L. Hnuni, "Ethnicity, Identity and Hermeneutics: An Indian Tribal Perspective," in *Ethnicity and the Bible*, ed. Mark G. Brett (Boston: Brill Academic Publishers, 2002), 348. (Original: J. Herbert Lorrain and F. W. Savidge, "After Ten Years: Report for 1913 of the BMS Mission in South Lushai Hills, Assam," in *The Annual Report of BMS on Mizoram 1901–1938* [Serkawrn: Mizoram Gospel Centenary Committee, 1994], 93–4.)

embracing of Christianity—indeed, it lives on today. Furthermore, the Christian observance of Sunday as a day of non-work chimed with the old tribal religious belief that some days were thought to be bad omen days.[64] In pre-Christian days, most tribal groups believed in "taboo days," when no one was allowed to travel or engage in work since it was believed that such actions could bring tragedy to the family or the entire village. Upon becoming Christians, to some extent even today, travelling on a Sunday or engaging in non-sacred tasks, such as opening shops, are held to invite tragedy, be inauspicious and against God's will.

Pre-Christian tribes also believed in some form of life after death and the existence of a "Village of the Dead" (*Misikhua* in Paite). Accordingly, when someone died, it was customary for the deceased to be buried with some personal items, as well as with basic items thought to be useful for their journey to the village of the dead. After conversion to Christianity, such customs remain, and some even place a Bible in the coffin along with the other items for the dead to carry on their journey. Rather than being seen as a living agent that invites personal engagement, the Bible was and is viewed as if it offers protection from danger and powerful, evil spirits.

The above discussion about continuities with pre-Christian times reveals that while ideological concepts were not adapted to achieve conformity with biblical teaching, outward changes, developments and improvements may be observable. In light of this, it is interesting to note that the perspectives and attitudes toward tribal women and their status seemed unchanged even though living conditions in general have improved with the coming of Christianity.

Why Are Women Still Subjugated After Embracing Christianity?

I think women's subjugation continued within tribal communities after they embraced Christianity not simply because such cultures are patriarchal, but precisely because women's subordination is believed to be and promoted to be the biblically ordained order. Such a belief seems to have been instituted in two ways: First, through utilizing patriarchal elements in the tribal society. Second, through the Christian missionaries themselves and the Christianity they brought being patriarchal. In other words, to take the case of the Paite tribe, the patriarchal society's placing of women in lower status—both in how they are perceived and in assigning secondary roles—found confirmation in the new religion they embraced, in how missionaries lived and transmitted Christianity.

---

64. Downs, "Faith and Life-style," 29–30.

Male-centric Term for God

I am convinced that one important factor that contributes to women's subordination as *the* Christian way or *the* biblical mandate is the adoption of male-centric terms and language in Christianity. One prominent example is the term for God, *Pathian*, where "Pa" is a masculine signifier. While no Paite Christian would claim that God is male or has a gender, the use of a masculine term for God inherently makes the association between being male and being the superlative figure and power. The term *Pathian* is the same as in Mizo, the language from which the Paite Bible was first translated.[65] As such, it is important to understand how this masculine term came to be adopted for God in the Mizo language.

In addition to the Paite and Mizo cultures being closely related, the first Paite Bibles were translated from the Mizo. Furthermore, the Paite tribe first received Christianity from Watkin Roberts, who was a mission worker in the Lushai hills among the Mizo people, and the native missionaries to the Paites were also Mizo converts. As such, in the earliest years of Paite Christianity, tribal converts would read the Bible in Mizo and sing Mizo songs. Paite Christianity surely was influenced by that of the Mizos, which in turn was from Western Christian missionaries.

Ralte's discussion about how *Pathian* came to be adopted as the Mizo term for God and how it enhances women's subordination in Mizo Christianity is truly eye opening. She persuasively argues that the missionary's choice of *Pathian* as the term to be used for the Christian God could not fully capture the essence of God in Mizo tribal understanding because *Pathian* is associated with the limited essence of the biblical God.[66] In indigenous Mizo tribal belief, *Pathian* (masculine) is the creator who lived far away in heaven and was inactive in the affairs of the people, while *Khuanu* (feminine) is believed to be the one who creates life and also ends it. *Khuanu* is like the primordial mother of every child born, always present with the people, giving protection, blessings and guidance

---

65. The Mizo Bible translation work was completed in August 1959, and the first full Paite Bible appeared in 1971. While I was unable to find written evidence related to the translation history, the fact that the first Paite Bibles as well as first hymns were translated from the Mizo was simply common knowledge, especially among older Church leaders. There are other important technical terminologies that Paite shares with Mizo, or perhaps adopted from Mizo, one such being *Sakhua* (spelled in Paite as *Sahkhua*), the term for "religion." There are also arguments that the term *Sakhua* itself originated from the god *Khuanu*, that is, the worship of *Khuanu*. Nowadays the term means "worship of divine" or simply "religion."

66. Lalrinawmi Ralte, "Patriarchy and Christianity in the Mizo Church: A Feminist Critique," *Bangalore Theological Forum* 31, no. 1 (1999): 117–33.

to the people. *Khuavang* (neuter) is the divine who focuses on help, care and blessings of the people.[67] Faced with these options and the dilemma to pick one term for God, Ralte argues, the patriarchy-oriented missionaries chose *Pathian* despite the disagreements among the three Mizo chiefs and other Mizo commoners who they consulted.[68] As such, the more inclusive understanding of God in indigenous tribal belief gradually became exclusively male oriented, and male superlatives came to predominate. All of this was a direct result of early decisions that the early missionaries made as they attempted to explain the Christian faith to the tribal people.

Now, while there are no known records of early Paite Bible translators struggling to choose a term for God—a problem that arose in the Mizo's case—the Paite had options when it came to finding a word to use for God—*Pathian*, a masculine word, and *Kouziin*, a neuter one. Given the closely similar cultures of Mizo and Paite, as well as the formative role of Mizo Christian converts within Paite Christianity, it would have been only natural and to be expected to use *Pathian* when translating the Paite Bible from the Mizo Bible. I think Ralte is right to highlight the missionaries' role in the transfer of the patriarchal system of Christianity to the Mizo tribes of Northeast Indian tribes—something that I believe can also be seen in the Paite context. In their enthusiasm to convert the people, the missionaries failed to take the time to study and understand how the tribal religion had both masculine *and* feminine/maternal elements in their belief systems.[69] As a result, the missionaries ended up imparting, at least partly, their own patriarchal ideologies rather than a genuine biblical one.

Re-examining Education, the Often Cited Evidence for Upliftment of Women

Another key factor in the persisting subordination of women is education—despite it often being cited as evidence for the elevation of women. I agree with Downs that most writers assumed, as he himself had done, that Christianity contributed positively to the advancement of women in the Northeast India, particularly through education.[70] Yet, while Christian missionaries were largely responsible for the introduction of female education, those same Christians for the most part excluded females from their mission and ecclesiastical systems. Remarkably, this situation continues

---

67. J. Shakespear, *The Lushei Kuki Clans* (Aizawl, Mizoram: Tribal Research Institute, 1975), 61. Also see: Ralte, "Patriarchy and Christianity in the Mizo Church," 121, 125, 127.

68. Ralte, "Patriarchy and Christianity in the Mizo Church," 127.

69. Ibid., 130.

70. Downs, *The Christian Impact on the Status of Women*, i.

up to the present day. In light of this, it is curious that missionaries bothered to work for female education and upliftment in the first place.

The missionaries' interest in female education was primarily the result of and influenced by women's movements that arose in Western countries from the late eighteenth century onwards—the very social contexts from which the missionaries came.[71] As such, the urge to work for the women in their mission field was not necessarily driven by theological convictions or a biblical basis. In fact, very few of the women missionaries were trained in theology, suggesting that their efforts in helping the girls and womenfolk of the mission field were actually the result of socio-cultural concerns.

Fundamentally, female education was still based on, and designed to serve, patriarchal norms. For instance, the earliest rationale used by the missionaries, such as the American Baptists, for educating girls was so that the men who were being trained for church leadership might have Christian wives.[72] In effect, the missionaries were concerned that the young men they trained would have to look for life companions among "their heathen countrywomen." And that was the motivation behind the missionaries and missionaries' wives providing education to the girls. In short, the girls were trained to be more effective homemakers. What this means is that the girls were seen as, treated as and taught to be subordinate to boys/males, and thereby trained to conform and do well in that status and role.

Barr, a historian of the medieval period, traces how the Christian definition of godly women as meekly accepting their subordinated status and position operated in the eighteenth and nineteenth centuries. Barr finds that this ideology of the godly woman's place being below that of men was not born out of theological or biblical concepts. Rather, it followed societal trends and movements such as the Enlightenment and Industrial Revolution which restricted women to domestic, household roles while raising men to public, ruling positions.[73] Directly or indirectly, the mission agencies that reached Northeast India subscribed to such definitions and

---

71. For a discussion of the rise of women's movements in the West and their relationship with missionary movements in the Northeast India see ibid., 30–41.

72. Ibid., 57.

73. In short, the Enlightenment's theory of complementarity argued that women were built for domesticity and child-rearing, while rule, rationality and public duties were for men. This was followed by the rise of modern science, which reinforced the biological differences between the sexes in order to argue for the appropriateness of women for domestic roles. Then followed the Industrial Revolution and its policy of paying women, the "weaker" sex, less than male factory workers. Beth Allison Barr,

characterization of gender roles. Consequently, the Christianity carried by the missionaries was primarily framed by their own ideologies and culture, such that the developments sparked by the new religion they brought involved elements of control and gender-specific expectations.

Education was also a means of forming a new elite for the tribal societies. This resulted in social imbalances that lingered on throughout the life of the imperial occupation, imbalances that became even worse after the departure of the British.[74] For example, those educated by missionaries and connected with the mission emerged as the most respected and powerful individuals within the Paite community.[75] The new elite comprised mostly, if not exclusively, men. Many of the school attendees became Christians and many of them went on to serve the mission; some would be recruited directly by the mission, and others would serve as volunteers.[76] As Basumatary spells out clearly, "For a talented young man, the favour of a Church could mean financial assistance to enable him to reach the threshold of higher education in the plains. The Church, thus, became a centre of power and patronage in the hill districts."[77] It was the men that the missions and then the Church invested in. In addition to being the primary religious and cultural agency, the Church often also became the principal employer of the people they educated, who were mostly boys/men. This is confirmed plainly by the lists of students in mission schools, which contain a disproportionate number of male names. The same is true for the lists of those employed by the missions and Church.[78] One obvious reason why fewer girls were sent to mission schools was because

The Making of Biblical Womanhood: How the Subjugation of Women Became the Gospel Truth (Grand Rapids: Brazos Press, 2021), 161–5.

74. Basumatary, *Ethnicity and Tribal Theology*, 84.

75. S. Thianlalmuan Ngaihte and Kaba Daniel, "Discourse on Tradition and Modernity Among the Paite," in *NEIHA: Proceedings, 32nd Session, 2011*, 560 (available online at https://papers.ssrn.com/sol3/papers.cfm?abstract_id=2173701).

76. For instance, in the Manipur hill area of Ukhrul, the Kuki tribe students who attended the mission school volunteered to transmit the new message to their own people, who were scattered all over the state. A similar case was seen in the neighboring region of Lushai hills. Dena, *Christian Missions and Colonialism*, 94–6.

77. Basumatary, *Ethnicity and Tribal Theology*, 85.

78. For example, the list of students attending the elementary school at Kaihlam village in 1919 mentions only boys. Liankhohau, *Social, Cultural, Economic and Religious Life*, 128. The lists of students and mission/church workers are similarly all male. Lalmuoklien, *Gospel Through Darkness: The History*, 80–2, 92–3. The list of students on p. 82 does contain some girls' names, but they are said to attend some "Girl's School" and "Midwifery School." Also, the natives employed by the Mission agency were all males. Dena, *Christian Missions and Colonialism*, 94.

the parents needed them to help with chores at home. A more important reason, however, was that the mission's main educational aim was to train and recruit leadership for the churches, to produce the teachers, evangelists and pastors who would form the backbone of the mission and ecclesiastical structure, which, of course, was exclusively occupied and controlled by men.

Patriarchally Structured and Controlled Missions
Essentially, a principal reason why the subordination of women continued among Northeast Indian tribes, even after conversion to Christianity, was because the Christianity brought to Northeast India by the missionaries inherently advocated a lower status for women. As Downs notes, the missionaries themselves were shaped by almost two thousand years of patriarchy in Jewish and Christian society, even though "there are, of course, important and even central elements in the Christian ideology that provide a rationale for absolute egalitarianism..."[79] The mission agencies were very effective in making the tribal churches and societies hierarchical, based on gender. The missions themselves seem to have followed the example of imperialist colonialists, who were, importantly, not biblically based or rooted. As Dena explains:

> The manner in which mission stations and church organizations were controlled, paralleled the colonial-bureaucratic structure. Colonial societies always acted as the model of a pyramid in which a minority at the top controlled large numbers at the base, with the aid of a medial cadre groups which manifested characteristics of both the rulers and the ruled. For example, if the colonial administrators governed through a native authority (tribal chieftainship), the missionaries also operated through a native cadre of teachers, evangelists, pastors and others.[80]

---

79. "All missionary societies were administered and controlled by men," at least until the early twentieth century. Thereafter, women at local churches began to appropriate the missionary cause for themselves, becoming informed about missionary works and raising most of the funds for mission activities. Gradually, women's missionary societies were formed, such as the first of its kind in America, the Women's Union Missionary Society of America in 1860. This mission sent out its first missionary to China in 1868. The American Baptists established a separate woman's missionary society in the United States, the Women's American Baptist Foreign Mission Society in 1871. In Britain, the Church of England Zenana Missionary Society was formed in 1880. Downs, *The Christian Impact on the Status of Women*, 36–9, 56.

80. Dena, *Christian Missions and Colonialism*, 100.

As the missions became firmly established and were handed over to the medial cadre of native workers, the native groups naturally followed the same hierarchical model of the mission structures. Women remained in the category of the large numbers at the base.

In sum, the tribal Christianity of Northeast India continued to subjugate women based upon the fact that the tribes were (in fact, still are) patriarchal, and the Christian missions themselves functioned patriarchally. The efforts towards advancement, including female education, can be seen to have operated within gendered parameters. The education of girls, while a positive development, was undertaken with the underlying acceptance that women were and should be subordinate to men. As such, the lower status of women/girls was not challenged, changed and affected, but rather became more deeply entrenched. Besides these two factors, there is one core element of Christianity that played a critical role in the establishment of women's status in tribal Christianity—the Bible.

The Place and View of the Bible in Tribal Christian Society

With the adoption of Christianity, the tribes also embraced the Bible and hold it to be precious, vital and highly significant. This is as it should be. Yet the Bible also seems to be perceived primarily as containing the "rules" of God, such that following them will "appease" God and thereby bring prosperity and protection. As Thanzauva and Hnuni assert, as "the most Christianized ethnic group in India," Northeast Indian tribal Christians are also "mostly biblicists who try to use the Bible as a magical book to solve their problems."[81] Evidently, the tribes accepted the Christian God mainly because this God was more powerful than the gods or spirits they had previously been worshipping. The Christian God was able to heal sicknesses that their former gods could not; this God could provide when their former gods left them starving in famine. Following such perceptions of God, the Bible also tended to be viewed as a replacement for the "magical" elements or spells used by pre-Christian priests to fight off troubles.[82] Except, the Bible is more powerful.

Seen as the substitution of the traditional charms which were used to ward off evil spirits, the Bible is carried on all journeys, offering protection from evil spirits.[83] This perception persisted even until recently. I remember how, growing up, we would put the Bible near our pillows so

---

81. Thanzauva and Hnuni, "Ethnicity, Identity and Hermeneutics," 343, 347.
82. Ibid., 347.
83. Downs, "Faith and Life-style," 30.

that ghosts or evil spirits would not dare to come near. The physical book was used as a protective shield. While this may sound amusing, such acts were done in all seriousness and reveal how the physical Bible was thought to have a special power, some sort of magical power. The Bible is also internalized and as such a profound component of the identity of the Christianized tribal societies.

The view that the Bible should be the guiding principle in a Paite Christian society is a common conviction. Since embracing Christianity, the Paite tribe has held up the Bible as central in their societal life and polity. As Siamkhum notes, the moral life of the society of the Paite is aimed and claimed to be based on biblical principles. "They [Paite Christians] use the Bible in their decision-making of moral questions. The Bible is their source of moral principles."[84] Their sincere yearning to be a biblical tribe and society shows up in a variety of ways and contexts. For example, the objective of the largest philanthropic organization of the Paite tribe, the *Young Paite Association* (YPA), is basically to promulgate and sustain Christian society. It states in its objective: "to adopt and impart to itself and the Paite people with the spirit of altruism in line with and in implementation of Christian values."[85] This objective continues today, whenever there are enough Paite people to form a YPA branch. To name one instance, in New Delhi, the capital of India, the YPA–Delhi Joint Headquarters states in its online declaration that it seeks to be "the sacrosanctity of Christian Values," with the objective "to encourage and promote a living according to the Christian tenets and teaching; to show respect to God the Almighty; stand up for truth; leading an exemplary life and communication through words that are acceptable to all."[86] It is clear that tribal Christians such as the Paite desire to utilize the Bible as their guide and basis for their governance. The critical question remains whether appropriate Bible study, aimed at understanding the biblical context and applicability in our modern lives, has been done.

Another area that shows the tribe's desire to align with the Bible is in how (some) Paite Zomi tribes have sought to assess their origin theories based on the Bible. One theory of their origin, the *Khuul* theory, posits that the Zomi originated from a pit somewhere in central China (*Khuul* is the Paite word for cave, pit or hole).[87] The *Khuul* theory of their origin is

---

84. Siamkhum, *The Paites: A Study*, 80.
85. The Young Paite Association was founded on March 3, 1953, *YPA Ki-ukna Daan Bupi: The Constitution of the Young Paite Association* (Churachandpur, Manipur: Young Paite Association, 2003 [amended]).
86. https://www.ypadelhi.com/dypa/ Accessed on March 8, 2022.
87. Kamkhenthang, *The Paite: A Transborder Tribe*, 1.

judged to be unrealistic and unacceptable because "the theory that a new civilization was restarted when men came out of the dark pit in the earth contradicts the biblical origin of man."[88] Another theory of the origin of the Zomi people, known as the biblical theory, traces them to Japhet, the third son of the biblical Noah.[89] Rejecting a theory based on the judgment that it is not biblical, and on the other hand trying to trace their origin directly to a biblical ancestor, simply reflects just how they desire to align with the Bible.[90] More importantly, it indicates how the biblical texts are easily read literally and applied directly/linearly in a simplistic manner without careful analysis of the biblical contexts and our modern lives.

Today, the view of the Bible among the Paite is predominantly one that places Scripture in high esteem. Most subscribe to the doctrine of inerrancy of the Scripture and the plenary verbal inspiration which accepts that every word and term, even numbers and grammatical tenses, are God-breathed and inspired. The most prominent and prevailing view of the Bible among the Paite is best captured in the doctrinal statement of the largest denomination of the Paite, the Evangelical Baptist Convention (with smaller denominations displaying no significant differences). It states, in translation:

> Holy Bible, thirty-nine books of the Old Testament and twenty-seven books of the New Testament, complete revelation of God, the only written word of God, every part of which is God-breathed, no error in its original manuscript, foundational for faith and daily life, essential to follow and to be used for final ruling.[91]

In expounding this statement of faith about the Bible, this declaration asserts that the very words of the Bible are themselves God's revelation.[92] The phrase "God-breathed" is explained as being the same as when God breathed into the nostrils of the first human, bringing life (in Gen. 2:7). And that is how the Bible became a word of life and living word.[93]

---

88. Siamkhum, *The Paites: A Study*, 20.

89. Ibid., 19.

90. Among different theories, the commonly accepted view, especially among the intelligentsia, is that their forefathers migrated from somewhere in China, through Myanmar, with some continuing on into the Northeast region of India.

91. *Evangelical Baptist Convention Thu-Upte* (Churachandpur, Manipur: Evangelical Baptist Convention, 1998), 1. This doctrine of the verbal inspiration of Scripture is also widely accepted by most, if not all, tribal churches in Northeast India. Thanzauva and R. L. Hnuni, "Ethnicity, Identity and Hermeneutics," 346.

92. *Evangelical Baptist Convention Thu-Upte*, 2.

93. Ibid., 5–6.

In explaining how the Bible was free of error in the "original autograph," it is clarified that the original or first manuscript is now beyond recovery. Be that as it may, the unavailability of the original manuscript does not invalidate the translated versions we have today from being inspired.

The above general perspectives of the Bible and the place of the Bible in the Christian tribal society are still prevalent and predominant today among the majority of Paites. A sample of the dominant views within the tribe, as well as some marginal views held by a few, can be observed from the responses I received during a recent survey I performed. All ten individuals who responded, five men and five women, are professing Christians, ranging from different areas of the society, six lay Christians (two not attending Church), four holding church leadership, four currently live outside of India, and two involved in some Christian ministries in multicultural contexts.[94]

On the question of whether our society outside the Church should base itself on the Bible, only two correspondents—one lay and one involved in the urban multicultural ministry setting—were of the opinion that our larger society should not base itself on the Bible. Another cautioned against making our biblical standards mandatory in general society. On the question of upholding the Bible as the ultimate authority, all denied that the Bible is being used as the ultimate authority in our Church and society, even though most affirm that our Church and society does claim it to be the ultimate authority.

One response was particularly revealing of the perplexing experience of tribal Christian women. The female responder compared what is being preached with her real-world experience. She stated:

---

94. These interviews were carried out between February 21, 2022 and March 5, 2022. The three main questions asked were: (1) Do you think our society (outside the Church) should base itself on the Bible and biblical values/teachings? Why or why not? (2) How should we understand and use the Bible? For example, as a rule book of God, or of the Church? Or can we treat it like a living book/organism so that we can discuss with or even question the Bible? If so, how? (3) Do you think you and/or our people believe in and use the Bible as the ultimate authority? If so, how to resolve when there are different interpretations? For example, our tribal Christian society is patriarchal (or perhaps complementarian)—that is, women are below men, and men should have the final authority both at home and at Church. However, some other Christian societies/communities are egalitarian—men and women are equal and mutual, so they have the same share in making final decisions at home and at Church. How would you respond to these two different or opposite kinds of Christian' biblical interpretations?

> I have not seen much dominance in the house, rather it was more of egalitarian where our men encouraged the women to be equally responsible for their rights. But then when it comes to differential of opinion, it was always the men that have the last say because they are either older or superior which is really hypocritic against the actual preaching… [S]o, in our real world, equality is fought for and encouraged, however ultimate authority when it comes to reality lies back to men. Why is that? Why does a family who does not have eligible men in the house, still need to find another (man/men) to speak on their behalf?

This responder's confusion about what is preached and her experience in real life is not uncommon. It shows the tension between biblical teaching and our Paite patriarchal practices. Two other responses, on the other hand, reflect the dominant view of the Bible in our church. Both responses came from women, committed church-attending Christians living in a tribal society with Paite majority in Manipur. One openly stated that "biblical teaching is the truth and completely without error and should be accepted and followed. While both men and women are saved in the same manner, when it comes to spiritual and physical ruling, men are given extra responsibility." The other expressed that "God says in the Bible that the helper of man is woman and being a helper is a great thing. Differential interpretations such as an egalitarian interpretation must have derived from personal wish and ego."

Finally, one respondent's statement captured well the challenge that our well-meaning efforts of being a biblical or Christian society face: "On the surface, our tribal society at large might still affiliate to the vaguely defined Christian culture." We look biblical on the surface, and we (can) define as Christian or biblical in a very vague way. We lack deep, critical study to define true biblical/Christian values and teachings. And the important question remains untreated: whether we are preaching and practicing what is truly biblical, whether we are really fulfilling what it takes to be biblical.

One significant thing I observe from the survey responses is that those who experience other (Christian) cultures are more sensitive to different readings of the Bible and reflective of the limitation of our own interpretation and application. On the other hand, those living within our own culture—tribe and church—tend to have a stronger, more rigid position on what the Bible is and what it says. Such rigid definitions are particularly prevalent when our own cultural norms are well-defined and broadly accepted. In such cases, the uncritical acceptance of these norms as biblically derived seems commonplace. I will come back to this topic in the concluding chapter, where I will also offer some guidelines about reading the Bible with sensitivities to other readings.

Brief mention may also be made of the origins of Paite Bibles. The first Bible in Paite was born when one of first Paite Christian leaders, Rev. H. Nengzachin, started translating the New Testament and Psalms. This first edition was then translated from the Mizo-language King James Version in 1944.[95] The second Paite Bible, which is the first complete one, *Laisiangthou*, came out in 1971. It was a translation of the Mizo Bible, which was itself a translation of the English King James Version.[96] There are important, theological/biblical words that the Paite shares with Mizo, such as the word for God, *Pathian*. This, as already mentioned, may be due to the fact that the Bible translation was undertaken by the first local missionaries who assisted the Western missionaries to the Paites, individuals who were Mizo converts.

The next Paite Bible version was completed thanks to the hard work of, and under the direction of, Rev. Jamkhothang Tombing. It was dedicated on February 5, 2005.[97] Another church leader, Rev. G. Khamkam, started translating the Bible into Paite in the 1960s; the work was completed and published by the Bible Society of India on December 7, 2008. A re-edited version was then published again in 2016 by the Bible Society of India. A new, revised translation is currently being undertaken by Rev. Kamkhenthang Mangte. The Paite Bibles were translated from other

---

95. Rev. H. Nengzachin was the first Paite to study theology abroad; he studied at the Eastern Baptist Theological Seminary (now called Palmer Theological Seminary) in Philadelphia, USA, from 1936 to 1939. Nengzachin was born on May 1, 1910 at Mimbung village, Mizoram; he died on November 12, 2003 at Lamka, Manipur, India.

96. Published by the Bible Society of India (BSI).

97. The history of this translation is as follows: Bibles International, the translation's publisher, adopted the Paite project in 1984. Along with editors from Bibles International, under the leadership of Dr. Henry Osborn (1924–2011), H. Nengzachin worked on a complete Bible translation. However, when Osborn discovered that the work done by Nengzachin was a word-for-word translation from the King James Version, a decision was made to start a new translation from scratch. Nengzachin, then, chose to resign from the project. Phaipi confirmed this information via the website of Bibles International, which he accessed on December 1, 2015 (http://biblesint.org/biNew/languages/asia-a-the-pacific-toptabs/paite). Phaipi, "Mission Transformation for Evangelical Baptist Convention," 41 n. 98, 100. While the above link is now no longer active, a similar historical account is recorded (without giving names) at https://biblesint.org/languages/patris (accessed April 2, 2022).

Rev. Jamkhothang was the then General Secretary of the Evangelical Baptist Convention, the largest denomination of the Paite tribe. Unfortunately Rev. Jamkhothang passed away on February 22, 2004, a year before the dedication of this Paite Bible, a project for which he worked very hard and which he eagerly wished to see bear fruit.

translated Bibles, the first two from Mizo and later ones from English. The main differences in the versions, apart from following their parent translations (Mizo or English), are to be found in the use of distinctive Paite language, notably the choice between older, more poetic language and more contemporary and vernacular expressions.

In sum, the following can be said about the place and view of the Bible in tribal societies. It can readily be seen that the Bible occupies a critical place in tribal Christian societies such as the Paite's, both in religious and secular institutions. The Bible is frequently held up and quoted by Churches and organizations as their guiding motto. Aligning with the Bible in all possible ways is yearned for. The Bible is also viewed mostly literally, as indwelled by some power, even magical power, to solve problems and almost as an absolute, unquestionable or non-discussable authority or law such that once the words "the Bible says…" have been uttered, what follows has to be accepted. Perhaps owing to—or rather perhaps in spite of—the special, vital and yet sometimes aloof position afforded to the Bible, proper and critical analyses of the biblical text tend not to be presented before it is applied to our modern-day contexts.

Conclusion

In this chapter, we surveyed the rich history and culture of the tribes of Northeast India and the various impacts British colonialism and Western Christian missionaries had on tribal communities. Substantial changes, such as the tribes losing their autonomy and being subjected to outside rule for the first time, affected many aspects of their interknitted communities, particularly how they relate among themselves. The traditional economy replaced by a money economy made men the main money earners and thus widened the gender gap and exacerbated issues of hierarchy. The new governance and economy of the tribes devalued women's contributions at home and within society since such things were not readily measurable monetarily. We also saw that while Christianity did help change and improve lifestyles and living conditions, most ideologies and customs have been retained.

The education brought by Christian missions is commonly and uncritically credited to have uplifted women. A careful study, however, reveals that the education system itself, just like the missions, was based on patriarchal foundations, underpinnings it worked to sustain. As such, the education offered by the missionaries rather contributed to the persistence and reinforcement of women's subordination. In other words, while the missionaries did not necessarily teach gender hierarchy or women's subordination as explicitly biblical, or as *the* Christian way, their own structures, systems and behaviors gave the impression that it was so. Upon witnessing this, the already patriarchal tribal cultures, including the Paite, upon accepting Christianity easily found affinities and reasons in biblical stories to validate their existing ideologies.

The critical place and high view of the Bible in tribal societies was also seen to contribute to the continued subjugation of women as biblical. It is undeniable that the tribal Christian Churches and societies, including the Paite's, aspire to be biblical in all areas of life. A such, it has been argued that it is crucial to study the Bible in its own context first, before extrapolating stipulations to be applied to our modern-day situations. In the following chapters we will study one of the most used Bible stories used to argue in favor of women's subordination being biblically prescribed, Genesis 1–3. Such a reading will be carried out by considering the text's own biblical context.

Chapter 3

CREATION OF HUMANITY IN GENESIS 1

Introduction

The account of the creation of humans in Genesis 1 may not be the most commonly or openly cited text to argue for women's subordination or gender hierarchy. It is, however, often considered and preached together with Genesis 2 and 3 by traditional tribal Christians such as the Paite to establish gender roles. For instance, in a recent denomination-wide "Dorcas" (women's group) Platinum Jubilee celebration, the executive head of the denomination preached that in Gen. 1:26, along with Gen. 3:16, God established gender roles in creation. The preacher opened by praising and crediting the women's group, proclaiming that "the great progress of the denomination is primarily because of the Dorcas group's hidden hard work and efforts." He went on to restate the widely known proverb, "Behind every great man there is a great woman."[1] The preacher

---

1. This sermon was at the Dorcas (Women group of the Evangelical Baptist Convention Church, EBCC) 42nd Annual Conference and Platinum Jubilee, held on November 28, 2021, at Churachandpur, Manipur, India. EBCC is the largest denomination among the Paite people. The speaker was the General Secretary of the EBCC. The sermon can be found online at https://www.youtube.com/watch?v=y4cLtthTyuA. The sermon starts at 2:20:40 in the video. The points noted above can be seen at 2:24:28, 2:27:23, 2:48:00 and 2:55:12. (Video accessed on March 28, 2022.)

The theme of the conference was "Return to Your Home/House," from Lk. 8:35, and so was thus the title of the sermon. The preacher was speaking mainly on the importance of starting at home/within the family even before trying to "fix" problems arising in wider community or society. While the whole sermon was not focused on gender roles, the speaker did highlight several times the rigid allocation of such roles, ones in which women are viewed simply as subordinate. Some examples are noted above in the discussion.

then cited Gen. 1:26 to claim that God made a family by creating male (Adam) and female (Eve), uniting them in marriage and blessing them to bear children and multiply and fill the earth. That is, God created the family unit at the very beginning of creation. The preacher continued with Gen. 3:16 (and also later mentions Eph. 5), explaining that when God told Eve that her desire would be her husband's, this is effectively God's establishment of the family order, with the man positioned at its head. He exemplifies his point by stating that in the case of godly people like Noah, Abraham and Jacob, the whole family obeyed whatever the father said and taught, and that this was how they became greatly favored by God.

Towards the end of his teaching the preacher exhorted the attendees to consider their own family arrangements, asking them to reflect on whether the fathers were playing their role as family leaders, with the women dutifully submitting to their husbands and taking care of their husband and children—for indeed, that is as it should be.

To be sure, what this denominational head preached was not a radical new concept or practice for the Paite tribal Christians. The gender and family order of male headship and ultimate authority and female subordinate status and helping role are widely and uncritically acknowledged, sincerely and strictly mandated for godly families and the wider society. The practice of male absolute authority and female subordination in tribal Christian societies is the accepted and promoted norm, one which is typically validated by citing the creation stories of Genesis 1, 2 and 3.

Indeed, Genesis 1, 2, and 3 follow the same theme throughout. But, contrary to the claims that Genesis 1, along with Genesis 2 and 3, embed women's subordinate status, a close study of the narrative demonstrates that male/man and female/woman are viewed and addressed together and neither gender hierarchy nor women's subordination are established. It is essential to closely examine the creation of humans in Gen. 1:26-28 in order to understand what is indeed established and what is not. As will be seen in the analysis below, noteworthy in the Genesis 1 account of the creation of humans is the fact that there is no explicit mention of gender hierarchy, or even of equality for that matter. But what is significant is that the male and female are addressed and viewed together throughout, without any hint of differentiation or ranking between them. Male and female are the same in their essence and nature of creation and are united in their purpose—both are created in the image of God and both are to fill the earth and rule over other creation. What the creation account of Genesis 1 establishes about humans is therefore the sameness and togetherness of male and female, rather than differentiation or order between them. To claim that there is a hidden or implied ontologically elevated leadership role given to the male over the female is to read our own extra-textual ideology into the text. Such a reading is unfaithful to the biblical text itself. The creation of humans in Gen. 1:26-28 will be comprehended better by studying the whole creation account of Genesis 1.

Purpose in Creation Account of Genesis 1

The creation of humans, found in just three verses of Genesis 1, is to be studied by situating it within the larger context of the creation narrative of Gen. 1:1–2:4a.[2] The creation account of Gen. 1:1–2:4a will be referred to in this study as "Genesis 1," for convenience. The final form of Genesis 1 will be analyzed here since it is a text with a unified literary form and structure as well as a coherent theme. Questions on sources, composition and redactional stages, such as whether and which ancient Near East creation account(s) was/were the original source or influence of this account in Genesis 1, and issues of redactional process, such as whether the text was composed or compiled by a single author/editor/redactor or some wider "school," are not necessary for the focus and argument of this study. Therefore, those discussions are not engaged with here. Furthermore, while I acknowledge the validity and credibility of assigning the creation stories to different authors, namely "Priestly" for Gen. 1:1–2:4a and "Yahwist" for Gen. 2:4b-25, the task in this study is not to analyze authorship. I concur with the opinion that the two creation accounts together in the final form narrate a canonical picture of creation, without contradiction in their themes, while they are different in literary style and emphasis.[3] The primary task here is to re-examine the presentation of male and female in the text, within its own context.

It is not hard for any reader to see that while the creation narrative of Genesis 1 is not detailed in itself, it does exhibit sophisticated literary patterns and features. The conciseness and lack of detail, however, seem

---

2. Genesis 1:1–2:4a, ending with the seventh day, is commonly accepted among Genesis scholarship as a literary unit for the first creation account, as can be seen in any critical Genesis commentary. For example, see E. A. Speiser, *Genesis*, AB 1 (New York: Doubleday, 1964), 8; Gerhard von Rad, *Genesis: A Commentary*, rev. ed., OTL (Philadelphia: Westminster Press, 1976), 45–6; Terence E. Fretheim, *Genesis*, *NIB* 1:340.

The chapter break in modern Bibles at 1:31, rather than 2:4, takes its cue from the medieval Vulgate translation (thirteenth century CE). See Bill T. Arnold, *Genesis*, NCBC (New York: Cambridge University Press, 2009), 29.

3. Fretheim, *Genesis*, 340.

to be purposeful. As von Rad argued, reading the account closely reveals it to be a carefully enriched doctrine of creation and the origin of the world, narrated in a deliberate, precise, symbolic, and comprehensive manner, utilizing just the essential elements to describe the created order.[4] In other words, what is mentioned in the biblical text is supplied purposefully; anything non-essential is left out. As such, it is necessary to resist the temptation to read our own ideologies or theologies into the text. With an utmost desire to stay true to the biblical text within its literary context, and with an awareness of our preconceived ideologies, we shall begin (re)reading the text of Genesis 1. The wider creation account will be considered first, drawing out regular patterns. Once this has been done, the creation of humans will be analyzed in closer detail.

Throughout the Genesis 1 account we find some consistent literary features appearing at each creation event, ones associated with the creation of each object or being. The first characteristic feature is that each day of creation is narrated in a pattern of announcement and execution.[5] After the introductory statement in Gen. 1:1-2, the six days of creation begin. Each day, and every event of creation, begins with an announcement of some form, typically the formulaic "God said," which is seen in 1:3 (Day one), 1:6 (Day two), 1:9, 11 (Day three), 1:14 (Day four), 1:20 (Day five), 1:24 and 1:26 (Day six). Each announcement is then followed by the actual events of creation. In most cases the creation is expressed as executed instantaneously, with the formulaic "And it was so" or "and there was" (in 1:3, 7, 9, 11, 15, 24), except for creation of sea creatures, birds and the human. The creation events of the living things, the sea creatures and birds (Day five, 1:20-23) and that of the human (Day six, 1:26-27) do not have the instantaneous execution expression "and it was so," but are rather supplied with other supplementary statements.

First, in the creation of living beings there is an additional "God created" or "God made" that follows the announcement of "God said." "God created" (*bārā*) is used for sea creatures and birds (1:21) as well as for the human (1:27), and "God made" (*'āśâ*) is used for the wild

---

4. Von Rad, *Genesis: A Commentary*, 47–8. Von Rad's observation about the deliberateness of the narrative, containing just the essential elements, is readily assessed as right by other scholars, such as Phyllis Bird ("'Male and Female He Created Them': Gen. 1:27b in the Context of the Priestly Account of Creation," *HTR* 74, no. 2 [1981]: 135) and David J. A. Clines (*On the Way to the Postmodern: Old Testament Essays 1967–1998*, Vol. 2 [London: Bloomsbury, 1998], 459).

5. This pattern or literary structure is widely recognized. For example, see Bird, "'Male and Female He Created Them'," 135.

animals (1:25) and for the human (1:26). Second, the creation of living beings is also supplemented with additional blessing statements. Living beings are blessed to increase and fill their habitats, the water and the earth (1:22, 28). Finally, the creation accounts of the living beings are also supplemented with "according to their/its kinds" (1:11, 12, 21, 24, 25), and for the human, the specification of "male and female" (1:27). Thus, all created things undergo the same patterns and processes, while all living beings receive supplementary blessings. This latter element effectively sets the living things apart from non-living entities, perhaps implying more intimate involvement from the creator God.

Another characteristic common to each of the creation events, including the creation of the human, is the presence of a coherent theme that runs throughout the creation account. That coherent theme is that the creation account of Genesis 1 establishes the purpose of each object or being created, purposes that can be identified as follows. The purpose of light, created on the first day, is to illuminate and to mark the day; thereby, the absence of light, that is darkness, marks the night (1:5). Expanse, created on the second day, is to function as the separator for the water above and the water below (1:6). The dry ground that appears on the third day after the gathering together of the water below, is to produce vegetation of plants and trees (1:11). The lights, created on the fourth day, are to mark the seasons, days and years, and to light the earth. The two lights are further differentiated into greater light, which is to rule the day and lesser light, which is to rule the night (1:14-16). Of the entities created on the fifth day, the water is to bring forth living creatures (1:20) and the land is to produce every kind of living thing (1:24). Similarly, the role for the human is to rule over other creatures, the fish of the sea, the birds of the sky, cattle, all the earth and all the crawling things on the earth (1:26, 28). Another theme of the creation account of Genesis 1 is the naming and establishment of function and purpose of each thing created. One thing the creation account of Genesis 1 tells us, then, is the purpose of the created humans, male and female. Importantly, there is no mention of any differentiation or ranking between them in their purpose.

Male and Female Together in Purpose
From the consistent, repetitive pattern in the creation account of Genesis 1 the purpose of the human is identifiable. The human is appointed to rule over other creatures and the earth. It is noteworthy that the plural is specifically used in this assignment of their purpose, implying that the male and female are together addressed and given the same purpose with the same responsibility. The plural is used in the announcement

of the creation of humans, followed by their subsequent purpose in Gen. 1:26 ("so that *they* may…"). Plural pronouns are used again in the reaffirmation of this purpose after they are created in 1:28 ("God blessed *them* and said to *them*…"; the verbs have plural endings too). These plural pronouns are in reference to the collective noun *'ādām* ("humanity," Gen. 1:26, 27) and also to the male and female named in the creation event (1:27). It is undeniable from the text that both male and female are together assigned the same purpose and responsibility. Nothing in the text states or suggests that either gender is to have primacy over the other. By implication and extension, then, both male and female mutually bear that given responsibility. It may be recalled here that considering the compact yet comprehensive literary nature of the narrative, if such order between the genders is an essential element of the created order, it would have been clearly expressed. Attempts to interpret that the male is given a higher status and authority, or a more important role, go beyond the biblical text.

In Paite tribal Christian society, which is patriarchal within the Church and its larger society, it is often said that male/man is created with higher status or ability, while female/woman occupy a lower or subordinated position. Strangely, such claims are made while fully accepting the statement in Gen. 1:26-27 to mean that both male/man and female/woman are equal and the same, being created in the same image and likeness of God. Yet, despite having a shared image and spiritual equality, so goes the argument, males are granted a God-given primary role, with females allocated a secondary role under the male headship.[6] The gender relation concept that the Paite Christians subscribe to is expressed precisely in Ortlund's argumentation. He argues for male primacy and headship over female by claiming that "God names the human race, both man and woman, 'man'," and that "God's naming the race 'man' whispers male headship… God did *not* name the human race 'woman'."[7] Yet, such claims are deeply flawed. They are not grounded on proper biblical exegesis, but rather on our own modern, cultural conceptions and the limitations of language. The error made in claims such as Ortlund's is that the argument is founded

---

6. Recall here, for instance, one of the survey responses mentioned in Chapter 2 (section "Place and View of the Bible in Tribal Christian Society") stating just this, that while both male and female are created equally in God's image and equally saved, male is given "extra" responsibility of leadership.

7. Raymond C. Ortlund, Jr., "Male–Female Equality and Male Headship: Genesis 1–3," in *Recovering Biblical Manhood and Womanhood: A Response to Evangelical Feminism*, ed. John Piper and Wayne Grudem (Wheaton: Crossway, 2021), 122–3 (italics original).

on the English language, not on the Biblical Hebrew. Ortlund seems to understand the word "man" in the particular English translation of Gen. 1:26-28—he cites from the Revised Standard Version—as referring principally to male human beings. Yet the term translated in this particular English version as "man," *'ādām* in the Hebrew, is actually a *collective* term for the whole human race, as has been recognized by many other English translations today, such as the New Revised Standard Version (NRSV), the New Living Translation (NLT) and the Common English Bible (CEB).[8]

Attempts are sometimes made to underpin the *'ādām* = "man/male" equation based on the observations that the Hebrew term is grammatically masculine and is sometimes used to refer to groups that are undeniably all-male. Yet this argument is undermined by the fact that Biblical Hebrew is an inherently male-oriented language. For example, the masculine term *'ādām* would be used to refer to a group of males *and females*, even when the males in that group are not necessarily leaders over the females in that group. The preference for the use of term *'ādām* is merely a symptom of how the Hebrew language functions. (The same phenomenon is seen in the French language, which would use the masculine form "ils" etc. when referring to a group comprised of, say, 99 woman and one man.) That a grammatically masculine term is used in the text of Gen. 1:26-28 is not evidence for male primacy, as can be seen clearly when examined in other languages, including the Paite language.

In Paite, the term for human is *mi* or *mihing*, with the terms for male and female being *pasal* and *numei*, respectively (*pa* is the masculine marker and *nu* the feminine marker). Importantly, the Paite word used to render Hebrew *'ādām* (human), *mi/mihing*, is a common noun, neuter in gender, inclusive of both male and female and leaning to neither gender. Therefore, in the Paite language, arguments in favor of male primacy deriving from the creation account of Gen. 1:26-28 are simply impossible. The *'ādām* = "man/male" linguistic support used by such interpreters as Ortlund simply does not hold. Fundamentally, such arguments are unsound and do not reflect the biblical message. It is to be noted that Ortlund's reasoning conveys precisely what the Paite community claims—male

---

8. That the term *'ādām* here is a collective noun referring to the whole of humankind as a species is widely accepted. See von Rad, *Genesis: A Commentary*, 57. For a fuller discussion on the term *'ādām* as referring to collective humankind, see David J. A. Clines, "אדם, The Hebrew for 'Human, Humanity': A Response to James Barr," *VT* 53, no. 3 (2003): 297–310.

headship is the norm, despite the clear assertion that male–female are made equal, being created in the same image of God and being authorized "male and female together to carry out the mission to rule the lower creation."[9] Such arguments result from entering the text with an already preconceived and accepted ideology of male headship. Such approaches stretch the text beyond what it actually says or implies.

As for the Paite Christians' arguing for male primacy on the basis of the Genesis 1 text, this is particularly puzzling when we recall that their own language prohibits such an argument. Such reasoning reveals how the Paite patriarchal culture and ideology is being read into the text, which does not hint at any male primacy or female subordination. In the text, it is key that male (*pasal*) and female (*numei*) are specifically named in being created in the image and likeness of God, without any hint of status or order between the two. As a matter of fact, even were only the linguistic equivalent to Hebrew *'ādām*, Paite *mihing*, used, it would still be correct to interpret the text as inclusive of both genders. Yet in specifically referring to male (*pasal*) and female (*numei*), any confusion and possible errors of interpretation are avoided. It is also worthwhile to consider that had the author intended to suggest order or hierarchy between the two, it could easily have been done, just as in the case of the assignment of roles for the lights.

In Gen. 1:16, it is stated that God made two great lights and the two are further distinguished as the greater light and the lesser light. Each of the two lights is also assigned a different role, while also being given the same general purpose of illumination. The greater light is assigned to rule the day and the lesser to rule the night. Now, one may argue that this distinction between the two lights is not sigificant and relevant to a comparison with the presentation of the human as male and female. Yet, the designation of one as "greater," with a particular assigned role, while the other is "lesser," and assigned a different role, is significant in that there is some sort clear sense of ranking and differentiation between the two great lights. This order is not nullified even if one translates the Hebrew words used in 1:16—*gādōl* and *qātōn*, "larger" and "smaller"— to be references to the respective physical sizes and/or intensities of the lights because a clear comparison or differentiation between the two still holds. Such a comparison or differentiation, however, is absent in the case of male and female humans. More importantly, the differentiation highlighted between the two lights reveals that where distinction is

---

9. Ortlund, "Male–Female Equality and Male Headship," 121.

intended it is indeed clearly expressed in the narrative. That both male and female are together in purpose, with no ontological male authority nor hierarchical distinction between the two being implied, will become even clearer when the details pertaining to the creation account of humans are considered.

Creation of Male and Female in God's Image
(Genesis 1:26-28)

Genesis 1:26-28 is a short account with repeated literary features and ideas that is otherwise devoid of details. Genesis 1:26 announces that God will create a human in God's image and likeness and that the human will rule over other creation. The announcement in 1:26 is executed in 1:27 and expands the human into male and female. Genesis 1:28 closes the account with God blessing them to multiply and fill the earth and commissioning them to rule over other creation. The creation of humanity in Genesis 1 is narrated concisely, just in three verses, vv. 26-28:[10]

> [26]And God said, "Let us make humanity in our image, according to our likeness so that they may rule over the fish of the sea, the birds of the sky, cattle, all the earth and all the crawling things on the earth."
> [27]So God created the human in his image
> In the image of God he created him
> Male and female he created them
> [28]God blessed them and God said to them, "Be fruitful and multiply, fill the earth and subdue it, rule over the fish of the sea, the birds of the sky and over all living things crawling on the earth."

The creation of humanity is carried out in a succinct and purposeful manner, as seen in this terse narrative. After creating the heavens and the earth and all the inanimate objects and living creatures (Gen. 1:1-25), in 1:26, God announces the intention to create yet another species, *'ādām*. We have noted earlier that the term *'ādām* is a collective noun referring to humanity, just like the term *mihing* in the Paite language. It is not a personal noun. God announces to make humanity in God's image and likeness without further explicating what that image and likeness are to be. The announcement to make humanity is fulfilled in the next verse, Gen. 1:27, where it is confirmed that both male, *zākār* (*pasal* in Paite), and female, *něqēbâ* (*numei* in Paite), are created in God's image. The closing

---

10. Translations here and elsewhere are mine, unless stated otherwise.

verse, Gen. 1:28, then concludes the creation narrative of humanity with a blessing to both the male and female to be fruitful and multiply, and with a reaffirmation of their purpose to rule over the other creatures. While the creation account of the first human follows similar patterns of the creation of all other objects, there are certain salient features unique to the creation of humanity.

"Let Us Make Humanity in Our Image and Likeness"
Following a similar pattern to that seen in other creation events, the creation of humanity also begins with the announcement "God said" (Gen. 1:26). Yet the account also has features not seen in the other creation events. The announcement continues with intimate, deliberate and intensive statements that are not supplied elsewhere (Gen. 1:3-25). The first feature in the unique divine speech that intrigues many interpreters is the use, in the original Hebrew, of plural pronouns for God (*'ĕlōhîm*). This demands a brief comment here.

In the Hebrew text God announces, "Let *us* make humanity in *our* image, according to *our* likeness" (1:26). The interpretation of the plural pronouns and verb ending (first common plural, *na'ăśeh*) by early Christian interpreters as referring to the Triune God or some polytheistic account are now dismissed on the basis that, on the one hand, trinitarian concepts were foreign to the original context and, on the other hand, Genesis 1 rejects polytheism.[11] In the context, the use of plural forms seems to imply some kind of announcement to the divine council, which is common in Old Testament understanding (see, for instance, 1 Kgs 22:19; Jer. 23:18-23; Job 38:7).[12] The use of the plural also connotes some deliberation, perhaps emphatic self-exhortation or intention, as indicated by the cohortative form.[13] That is, the divine announcement of the divine's intentionality is to create a being that will be unique, resembling and representing the creator in the created world.

It should also be noted that the use of the plural for God is not to be equated with the male and female differentiation of human created in God's image. God is neither male (*pasal*) nor female (*numei*), nor a combination of the two genders. That is, God's image is not to be understood in the sense of a physical replica, either male or female, because

---

11. Gordon Wenham, *Genesis*, WBC (Dallas: Word Books, 1987), 27–8.
12. Ibid., 28; Nahum Sarna, *Genesis*, JPS Torah Commentary (Philadelphia: Jewish Publication Society, 1989), 12; Fretheim, *Genesis*, 345.
13. Arnold, *Genesis*, 44.

in Israel's understanding, God transcends the sexual polarity that characterizes the creaturely world.[14] The human created in God's image and likeness being identified and differentiated as male and female is not an explanation of the nature of God but of the human. As God's image and likeness, humanity is like God and resembles God; and in that same essence, humanity is not God, only *like* God.

The other feature that has invited wide interest and numerous varied interpretations is the meaning of the "image" and "likeness" of God in which the human is (to be) created. The interpretations of "image" and "likeness" have been widely diverse, perhaps because the immediate context offers no further explanation about the terms as well as no description of God, the subject of the terms "image" and "likeness."[15] Common interpretations of the "image" and "likeness" include non-physical qualities such as human's mental and spiritual faculties, reasoning, personality, freewill, self-consciousness or intelligence. In the ancient Israelite concept, however, there is no marked differentiation of the physical realm and the spiritual/psychological, so these cannot be the original meaning.[16] A better understanding of the basic meanings of the terms will help in our appreciation of what being God's image and likeness entail.

The term "image" (*ṣelem*) basically means something cut out, an idol, a model (1 Sam. 6:5, 11; Amos 5:26; 2 Kgs 11:18; Num. 33:52), and the basic meaning of "likeness" (*dĕmût*) is similitude of appearance, lookalike (Ezek. 1:5, 26; 8:2; 2 Kgs 16:10).[17] The two terms work together to produce a more concrete sense of the whole being of human, rather than just one side, physiology or psychology. The terms basically mean a representation, like a model that stands for and bears the resemblance of the original. As such, while the text does not spell out the exact way(s) in which the human resembles God, it does point to the reason why the human is created in God's image and likeness. The human is to be made in the image and likeness of God mainly to serve a purpose, to rule over the other creatures and the earth as God's representative on earth. Therefore,

---

14. F. J. Stendebach, "*ṣelem*," *TDOT* 12:394.

15. The widely varied interpretations of the "image" and "likeness" are numerous and cannot be reviewed or listed with justice here. A summary survey of the different interpretations has been made by others, for instance, see Clines, *On the Way to the Postmodern*, 2:448–56.

16. Wenham, *Genesis*, 29.

17. BDB, 198, 853.

the notion of humanity bearing God's image is one of function rather than of substance.[18]

That being created in God's image and likeness implies purpose is also clear from the grammatical sequence of the jussive cohortative form followed by the unconverted imperfect form.[19] In addition, the fact that the phrase "rule over" is the only directly expressed factor connecting humanity and their being made in God's image and likeness suggests purpose. This meaning of the "image and likeness of God" as implying God's representative in ruling over other creation correlates with what we have observed about the coherent theme of Genesis 1, that is, naming the purpose of each created object or being.[20] In that connection, it may be stressed here again that the use of plurals in expressing the purpose of humanity ("so that *they* may rule…") implies that the male and female are together in this same purpose of ruling. No one gender takes a primary role over the other.

Beyond saying that humans are to *rādâ*, essentially "rule," over the non-human world, no further details are given in the Hebrew text. However, it can be reasonably assumed that as representatives of God the creator, they would be expected to rule as the creator God would. The term *rādâ* in other parts of the Old Testament is generally used in contexts where someone, often a king, or some nation rules over another individual, people or nations (Lev. 26:17; Num. 24:19; Pss. 72:8; 110:2; Isa. 14:2; Ezek. 29:15). As such, *rādâ* implies ruling by someone/something in authority, of superior position. Yet, it is also often associated with the exhortation or rebuke not to rule harshly or ruthlessly (Lev. 25:43, 46, 53; Ezek. 34:4). Thus, the term "rule" can be understood as indicating the assigning of the human a status higher than other creatures—the fish, birds, animals, the earth, that is, the non-human world.

---

18. Theodore Hiebert, "'God Saw How Beautiful It Was': Creation in the Bible as Science, Art, and Theology," in *The Earth is the Lord's: Essays on Creation and the Bible in Honor of Ben C. Ollenburger*, ed. Ryan D. Harker and Heather L. Bunce (Philadelphia: Eisenbrauns, 2019), 14.

19. The sequence of cohortative (here, "Let us…") and unconverted imperfect (of the verb *rdh*, "rule") connotes purpose or result. See Thomas O. Lamdbin, *Introduction to Biblical Hebrew* (1973; 19th Printing, London: Darton, Longman & Todd, 2009), 119.

20. This sense of purpose, the purpose of being God's earthly representative, implied in humanity being created in God's image, is expressed well in the CEB translation: "*so that* they may rule over the fish…"

At the same time, being given such a status and responsibility does mean humans are free to rule in any way they like—harshly or ruthlessly. Rather, as representatives of the creator God, they would be expected to rule and take care as the creator God would. Every human, both male and female, being created in God's image and likeness, are equally tasked with that responsibility.

Male and Female He Created Them

In the next verse, Gen. 1:27, the intentionality announced in the previous verse is fulfilled—the human is specified into male and female. However, in identifying the human into the two genders, male and female, no differentiation is made between them in the text—both male and female are each fully the image of God. The plural in the third line of v. 27, "…he created *them*," is contrasted with the singular in the previous line of the same verse, "…he created *him*," which prevents the reader from assuming the creation of an originally androgynous man.[21] Additionally, while the singular "him" of the middle line of the same v. 27 is grammatically masculine, it is not so ontologically[22] and it should be easily understood that it is referring to the collective noun *'ādām/hā'ādām* (*mihing*, "humanity/the human") referenced earlier. Specifically using the plural pronoun alongside specifically naming male and female substantiates that the *'ādām/hā'ādām* is certainly and irrefutably referring to both genders. It follows, then, that both genders are the same in their essence and nature.

By identifying the human as male and female the narrative makes manifest that the sexual distinction of the created order does not come at the expense of subordinating one to the other. To borrow von Rad's expression, "by God's will, man was not created alone but designated for the 'thou' of the other sex."[23] And *vice versa*. That is, in creating humanity, mutuality and togetherness—as opposed to differentiation—is the essence since creation. While the male and female are distinct, there is no differentiation between them in their purpose of being God's image and being God's representative. As Trible argues, the parallelism between the *hā'ādām* ("the human") and "male and female" in Gen. 1:27 shows

---

21. Von Rad, *Genesis: A Commentary*, 60.
22. Robert Alter, *Genesis: Translation and Commentary* (New York: W. W. Norton, 1996), 5.
23. Von Rad, *Genesis: A Commentary*, 60.

that the sexual differentiation means not hierarchy but rather equality.[24] Neither is made superior or subordinate, and neither is granted power over the other.

To further substantiate how the male and female are viewed and treated together in the text of Genesis 1, it is worthwhile to consider briefly how the concept of the "image of God" (*ṣelem 'ĕlōhîm*) functioned in the ancient Near Eastern world. In the larger ancient Near Eastern context, of which the creation account of Genesis is a part, the phrase "image of God" is associated with a royal ideology.[25] Particularly in Egyptian creation myths, it is the pharaohs, not common human beings, who are the bearers of the image of a deity. However, in Genesis 1's account of human creation, *all human beings* are the image bearers and thereby representatives of God, not just the kings or a select group of humans. And the human specified into male and female clearly indicates that both genders equally bear the image of God, are equally God's representative in the created world and are to work that out together in mutuality. There is no hierarchical ordering between the two genders. Additionally, it is also known that in Mesopotamian creation ideologies,[26] human beings were considered to have been created with the express purpose of being the slaves and servants of the gods. In contrast, in Gen. 1:26-28, far from being created to be slaves for God, the male and female are created to occupy the unique position as God's own representative on the earth. Once again, noteworthy here is how no differentiation is made between the male and female—both are equally and together given the "unique position" of being and ruling in God's place. The blessing statement in the following verse continues with the same theme and tone.

The creation event of the human concludes with another statement where God pronounces blessings on both male and female and reinstates the purpose of their creation in God's own image. As in the case of the announcement of the creation of human and their purpose to rule the non-human world together (Gen. 1:26), in the blessing and reassertion of their purpose too, plurals are used (1:28). The use of plurals in the Hebrew cautions against interpreting it to imply differentiation and/or the establishment of a hierarchy between the male and female human. Both male

---

24. Phyllis Trible, *God and the Rhetoric of Sexuality* (Philadelphia: Fortress Press, 1978), 17.

25. The "image of God" as royal ideology is a widely accepted concept among scholars. Bird, "'Male and Female He Created Them'," 140.

26. Ibid., 144.

(Paite *pasal*) and female (Paite *numei*) are equally blessed to be fruitful and multiply, and both are equally commanded to fill the earth, subdue it and rule over other creation. What does this mean for us today?

For a traditional tribal Christian society like the Paite's, the creation account in Genesis 1 teaches us that our claim that both males and females are equal, both being created in the same image of God, is substantiated by the biblical text. That is, the text grants no one gender a claim on ultimate authority over the other. Rather, the genders are united in having been uniquely tasked to be God's representatives, as "rulers" over other creatures of/and the earth. By extension, the roles of male and female humans are parallel, mutual and united. What the text of Gen. 1:26-28 emphasizes is sameness, togetherness and mutuality in fulfilling the human purpose to be God's representative within and amongst the wider creation—other humans included. Clearly, in being distinctively identified as male and female, they are not identical. Yet the text does not provide any hint of inequality between them in status or power in fulfilling the blessings and purpose given to them.

Admittedly, one can claim the precise opposite can be argued—that there is no unambiguous message of sexual equality present in the biblical text. Certainly, there are indeed no such explicit statements. Furthermore, as Bird notes, one may advocate for males being the primary gender and the determining image of humanity in Gen. 1:26-28 by drawing implications from later narratives. For instance, by reading these verses along with Gen. 5:1-2, where the creation of human account is repeated in the introduction of genealogies of Adam, or with Gen. 9:1, where the blessings of Gen. 1:28 are repeated in the blessing of Noah and his sons, or in light of the general tendencies for men to dominate in biblical genealogies,[27] one might construct fragile arguments to support a supposed overriding sense of biblically ordained male primacy. To such claims, it can be responded that the fact that men are made primary in later narratives and genealogies about ancient Israel does not establish a gender hierarchy for humanity. Male predominance in ancient Israel's genealogies is rather, I would argue, reflective more of the patriarchal culture in which such genealogies arose, and not representative of a biblical standard.

What is more significant is that in the very first account of human creation in the Bible, the establishment of maleness and femaleness comes about with a total lack of any hint of male primacy. Notably, subsequent to their being named and set apart, in Genesis 1 the male and female

---

27. Ibid., 151.

are always treated and addressed together throughout. Crucially, if male primacy was the intended biblical or universal order, it would certainly have been laid out in the creation account. Yet it was not. As Bird rightly concludes, the division of labor, honor and responsibility between genders is not a matter of the biblical creation account (Gen. 1); such concerns belong rather to later history[28]—and, we might add, to historically and geographically distanced cultures.

All considered, then, the creation account of Genesis 1 nullifies the arguments for male primacy and women's subordination as established "since the beginning of creation." At the very least, in specifically naming both genders and treating them together throughout, no hierarchy or ordering is established.

Conclusion

Genesis 1 is a text that cannot and must not be used in ontological arguments in support of women's subordinate status. The clear statement that humanity was created in God's image and likeness, and that male and female alike were equally tasked with being God's representative, jars strikingly with any argument of male primacy and female subjugation that seeks to claim support from Genesis 1. And yet "since creation" are words still used in such arguments, and are propagated in such contexts as traditional Paite tribal Christianity. A re-examination of the text of the creation account in Genesis 1, particularly of the human creation account in Gen. 1:26-28, reveals that there is no language or evidence of gender hierarchy in the biblical text. Being created in the same image and likeness of God, both male and female are together and equally assigned as representatives of God in the non-human created world. The use of plural pronouns in reference to humanity in Gen. 1:26, as well as the plural verb endings used in the blessing of male and female humanity and the assigning of their purpose in Gen. 1:28, also confirm their togetherness and the absence of setting one gender over another. Any implication of women's subordination must have come from external preconceived ideologies being read into the text.

For a traditional patriarchal culture such as the Paite tribe, then, a critical observation can be made. Our claims that male/man (*pasal*) and female/woman (*numei*) are both created equal in the same image and likeness of God, and our preaching and practice of women's subordination

---

28. Ibid., 157.

as if it is the biblical order since creation, become contradictory. While viewing and placing women in subordinate status may be our culture, it cannot be supported on biblical grounds since the text simply does not advocate that position. In short, sameness, togetherness and mutuality of the male and female are what are evident and emphasized in the text, not differentiation or hierarchical ordering. In fact, the common theme of sameness and togetherness also continues in the creation narrative of Genesis 2 and the "fall" account of Genesis 3, as we shall see in the next chapters.

Chapter 4

CREATION OF THE FIRST HUMANS IN GENESIS 2

Introduction

Genesis 2 is liberally quoted by preachers and lay tribal Christians alike to advocate women's subordination and male primacy as biblical. Unlike Genesis 1, which is analyzed in the previous chapter, Genesis 2 narrates the creation of humanity in a detailed way, with elements readily utilized by interpreters to back up their arguments for gender hierarchy. One of the key phrases in Genesis 2 that has been interpreted to subjugate women is *'ēzer kĕnegdô*, mostly understood to mean the first woman was created to be the helper for the first man (Gen. 2:18). In a tribal Christian society like the Paites', this phrase is an often-cited basis for arguing that women are subordinate to men since, the argument goes, they are created to be helpers for men. Hangzo expresses well the position of Paite (Zomi) tribal women when she writes: "Woman is considered as a helper to man, as 'Eve' was to 'Adam,' and her full membership to the family she marries into is completed once she bore a male child to continue the family lineage."[1] Or, as one woman assuredly stated in an interview I carried out recently, "God says in the Bible that the helper of man is woman and being a helper is a great thing. Differential interpretations such as an egalitarian interpretation must have derived from personal wish and ego."[2] The predominant view of man and woman in Paite society is captured clearly in Ortlund's argument: "A man, just by virtue of his manhood, is called to lead for God. A woman, just by virtue of her womanhood, is called to help for God."[3] The nub of the question, however, is whether the term in

---

1. Hangzo, "Gender Equality Among the Zomis," 54.
2. I describe this interview in detail in Chapter 2, under the section "Place and View of the Bible in Tribal Christian Society."
3. Ortlund, "Male–Female Equality and Male Headship," 102.

the biblical text institutes women's subordination, or whether readers are rather reading pre-existent ideology and pervading culture into the text. As such, it is imperative to re-examine the biblical narrative closely in its own context.

A literary analysis of Genesis 2 reveals that there is no establishment of women's subordination in the narrative, as will be demonstrated below. Terms and details from Genesis 2 that are variously used to argue for women's subordination include "helper" (Gen. 2:18, 20), man being created first and woman created from the man's body part (Gen. 2:7, 21, 22), and the man naming the woman (Gen. 2:23). Instead of differentiation or hierarchical ordering, in its context these terms and details emphasize the sameness and togetherness of the man and woman, who are seen and treated together as a pair or as partners throughout. Considering how subordination of women today is often attributed to the Hebrew phrase *'ēzer kĕnegdô* ("helper"), it is appropriate to begin our analysis of Genesis 2 by re-examining this phrase.

Meaning of the Phrase 'ēzer kĕnegdô

The creation of the first man and woman is narrated in Gen. 2:4-25.[4] For convenience, the narrative of the creation of humanity in Gen. 2:4-25 will be referred to in this study as the Genesis 2 creation account. The phrase *'ēzer kĕnegdô* (Gen. 2:18, 20) is translated variously as: "a help meet for him" (KJV), "a helper suitable for him" (NIV), "a helper as his partner" (NRSV), "a suitable partner for him" (NAB), "a fitting helper for him" (NJPS), or "a helper perfect for him" (CEB). As seen in these few examples, the translations of the phrase themselves do not appear negative or subordinating, so it seems that the argument of subordination for the woman from this phrase arises solely from the interpretation of the term "helper." Importantly, the meaning of the Hebrew term has to be considered within the wider textual context in which it appears; in an of itself, the term does not carry a well-defined meaning that can simply be plucked out and interpreted.

In Paite Bibles too the translations of the phrase *'ēzer kĕnegdô* are fairly unbiased and not conspicuously negative or subordinating towards the "helper" woman. The phrase is translated variously as:

4. It is widely accepted that Gen. 2:4-25 forms a literary unit, with the phrase "these are the generations of..." in the first part of 2:4 introducing the narrative that follows (cf. Gen. 6:9; 10:1; 11:10; 25:12, etc.). See, for instance, Wenham, *Genesis*, 55–6, and J. Andrew Dearman, *Reading Hebrew Bible Narratives* (Oxford: Oxford University Press, 2019), 149–51.

amah panpih ding a kithuahpih dia kilawm (older version)
"a suitable companion to help him"

a kituak huhmi (2004 version)
"a fitting helper"

amah toh kimil, a panpihtu ding, a kithuahpih ding (2008 version)
"a match with him, to be a helper, to be a companion"

amah panpihtu ding a kilawm (2016 version)
"suitable to be his helper"

As can be seen in these translations, the phrase contains the description of the kind of "helper" the woman would be—none of which convey any sense of lower status. As such, if read on its own terms, the phrase as a whole conveys more of a neutral or positive value, despite the negative or subordinating tone readers tend to read into it. The association of women as subordinates in this phrase seems to come from our prejudged and pre-allocated place of women in our minds and societies. As an illustration, the Paite term for woman, *numei*, already carries a subordinating sense. "*Numei*" is a combination of two words, *nu* and *mei*, where the first part, *nu*, is a feminine marker, and also means "mother." *Mei*, the second part, means "maid" and also means "concubine." While boy/man has (relatively more) freedom at home and in society, a girl/woman is bound by social "dos" and "don'ts," and there is no compromising for girls/women on their domestic chores. It is as if all household chores are reserved exclusively for girls/women—and thus off limits to boys/men. Girls/women are to live up to, embody, the role inherent in their name, *numei*. Whenever judged as saying or doing something considered not "girly" or feminine according to the societal or godly standard, a woman can easily receive the derogatory label *numei mei*—which is a way of saying, "you are just a girl/women—how would you dare?" *Numei mei* implies strong disapproval and disdain.[5] Such an embedded ideology and attitude in the identification of females/women can easily govern one's reading of a phrase like *'ēzer kĕnegdô*, used for the woman in Genesis 2, and the neutral or positive sense of the phrase can be missed.

While the above translations of the phrase *'ēzer kĕnegdô* in themselves, in English and Paite, do not imply subordination, these few examples also plainly show the challenge of translating the exact meaning of the phrase. As Robert Alter, a distinguished translator of the Hebrew Bible, succinctly

---

5. In other words, the expression *numei mei* means "you are a just a girl/woman, don't even think about it!" Ninglun Hanghal, "A Gender Perspective on Democratisation," in Ngaihte and Guite, eds, *Democratisation Process in North-East India*, 75.

summarizes, this phrase is "notoriously difficult to translate... 'Help' is too weak because it suggests a merely auxiliary function, whereas *'ezer* elsewhere connotes active intervention on behalf of someone, especially in military contexts, as often in Psalms."[6] Alter translates the phrase as "a sustainer beside him," which conveys the essence of the phrase more clearly. Zevit translates the phrase in a more literal way as "a helper like his kin."[7] In an attempt to encompass the sense of similarity between the man and the woman embedded in the phrase I also translate *'ēzer kěnegdô* more literally, as "a helper like his self." Thus, in Gen. 2:18 I read: "And YHWH God said, 'It is not good for the human to be alone; I will make him a helper like his self'."[8]

Let us re-analyze the phrase *'ēzer kěnegdô,* "a helper like his self," carefully in the original language, Hebrew. The phrase in the original carries a sense of similarity rather than hierarchy. The entire phrase is composed of a noun *'ēzer* and a compound word *kěnegdô*. The noun *'ēzer*, which translates basically as "helper, help, succor," mostly refers to God (Exod. 18:4; Deut. 33:7, 26, 29; Pss. 20:3 [20:2 Eng.]; 33:20; 70:6 [70:5 Eng.]; 115:9, 10, 11; 121:1, 2; 124:8; 146:6 [146:5 Eng.]; Hos. 13:9), though it can also refer to humans (Isa. 30:5; Ezek. 12:14; Dan. 11:34). Because *'ēzer* commonly refers to God, scholars such as Trible argue that *'ēzer* is a superior individual, and thereby the woman in Genesis 2 is not inferior but rather superior.[9] On the other hand, from the Hebrew usage of the verb *'āzar* ("help") from which the noun *'ēzer* derives, Clines argues that helpers are inferior, even when the verb is used in reference to a superior king or to someone with better and unique skills, or even to God. This biblical usage of the term and the above-mentioned opposing interpretations of it prove that the term itself does not inherently carry connotations of inferiority/superiority.[10] While the term is indeed used with God as the subject, that cannot directly imply superior quality when used for humans. God and human in biblical understanding cannot be simply equated.

The claim that the term always connotes inferiority is a stretch. According to Clines, *'ēzer* implies inferiority because in helping someone the helpers subject themselves to a secondary, subordinate position to

---

6. Robert Alter, *The Hebrew Bible: A Translation with Commentary*. Vol. 1, *The Five Books of Moses* (New York: W. W. Norton & Co., 2019), 14 n. 18.

7. Ziony Zevit, *What Really Happened in the Garden of Eden?* (New Haven: Yale University Press, 2013), 244.

8. This and other translations are my own. I offer word-by-word translations, rather than interpretive renderings, in order to aid the analysis of the verse in question.

9. Trible, *God and the Rhetoric of Sexuality*, 90.

10. As also propounded by Zevit, *What Really Happened?*, 127.

do something that is not their work but rather the job of the ones being helped.[11] Now, as Clines himself notes, when the king of Gezer came to help, "the Lachishites were presumably already doing all they could to resist the Israelites" (Josh. 10:33). Also, in battles it is always an outsider "who is 'helping' those with the problem on their hands" (2 Sam. 8:5; 1 Kgs 20:16; 1 Chron. 12:22 [12:21 Eng.]; Isa. 30:7).[12] So, in these cases, help from someone with higher ability—strength, power, skill—is necessary. It is questionable, then, to argue that there is necessarily a lowering of status/subordination involved in "helping." There are kinds of help that only God or a king can perform. Furthermore, were a king to become inferior by supplying help to a subject, he would effectively lose his kingship and thereby no longer have the authority or ability to help. Likewise, in helping humans, God does something humanly impossible, something that only a being superior to humans can do.

Webb points out that while most uses (72%) of the term *'ēzer* refer to someone with superior status helping one from a lower status, in about 18% of cases the "helper" is of equal status, and in just 10% the "helper" is of lower status.[13] If one is to argue from the term itself, then, the primary connotation of the term "helper" is one involving a superior status. Thus, while it is tempting to validate women's subordination as biblical from the woman as "helper" in Gen. 2:18, the term *'ēzer* does not designate a subordinate status. For a better understanding we need, then, to look at the phrase in which *'ēzer* appears.

The next element of the phrase in Gen. 2:18, *kĕnegdô*, is composed of the preposition *kĕ*, the noun *neged*, and the pronominal suffix *ô*. The term *neged* indicates locality and proximity—that is, physical nearness, being in front of or opposite to (Gen. 31:32, 37; 47:15; Josh. 3:16; 1 Kgs 21:13). The term also denotes "constant presence physically or mentally." We see this in numerous biblical texts: in Ps. 38:18 (38:17 Eng.), where pain is always with/before the psalmist; in Ps. 44:16 (44:15 Eng.), where disgrace is with/before the psalmist; in Ps. 51:5 (51:3 Eng.), where sin is with/before the psalmist; and in Exod. 10:10, where Pharaoh claims evil (plan) is with Moses. The noun *neged* thus gives a picture of the *'ēzer* ("help/helper") and the *'ādām* ("human") alongside each other, as together constantly, perhaps even beyond physical proximity. With the preposition

---

11. David J. A. Clines, *What Does Eve Do to Help? And Other Readerly Questions to the Old Testament*, JSOTSup 94 (Sheffield: JSOT Press, 1990), 30–2.

12. Clines, *What Does Eve Do to Help?*, 31.

13. The term occurs about 128 times (noun and verb forms taken together) in the Old Testament. William J. Webb, *Slaves, Women & Homosexuals: Exploring the Hermeneutics of Cultural Analysis* (Downers Grove: InterVarsity Press, 2001), 128.

kĕ ("as, like"), the noun *neged* conveys a sense of "similarity or being," of "correspondence" between the *'ēzer* and the *'ādām*. And with the pronominal suffix *ô* ("his"), that similarity or likeness is reinforced. Therefore, this compound term *kĕnegdô* in Gen. 2:18 carries the sense of "corresponding to him, that is, equal and adequate to himself,"[14] which may be literally translated as "like his self." The phrase does not express subordination or differentiation, but rather connotes close similarity and togetherness. While up to this point in the narrative it is not clear who the *'ēzer kĕnegdô* will be, it is clear that it will be a being of some similarity/sameness who could be together with the first, lone, human.

Creation of the 'ēzer kĕnegdô *(Genesis 2:19-23)*

YHWH God declares that it is not good for the human (*'ādām*) to be alone, though no reason for this is provided (Gen. 2:18). YHWH God then forms animals and birds and brings them to *'ādām* to be named. None of these creations is fit to be the "helper like his self" (*'ēzer kĕnegdô*) for the human (2:19-20).[15] As shown above, the phrase *'ēzer kĕnegdô* implies similarity and togetherness with the first human. It seems, then, that among the animals and birds there is not one like the first human that can offer sameness and proximity. God then began to create another being, another human, the woman (Gen. 2:21-22).

Man Created First; Woman Created from Man

Another argument that is often made for women's subordination is that the first woman was created *after* man and *from* man. The argument for men's higher status from being created first derives from the primogeniture tradition of tribal culture, such as the Paite's as well as ancient Israel's.[16] Following primogeniture tradition, which confers a leadership role to firstborn sons, it is inferred that the first man has higher status than the

14. BDB, 617.

15. It is also not stated in what way the animals and birds are not fit to be the *'ēzer kĕnegdô* for the human, at least not explicitly. The difference given in the narrative between the creation of animals and of the human is that while God breathed breath of life into the human's nostrils and formed the human from the dust (*'āpār*) of the ground (*'ădāmâ*), for the animals it is only stated that they are formed from the ground (*'ădāmâ*); the same verb, *yāṣar*, is used for forming both the animals and the human (Gen. 2:7, 19).

16. See, for instance, Wayne Grudem, *Evangelical Feminism and Biblical Truth: An Analysis of More Than One Hundred Disputed Questions* (Wheaton: Crossway, 2012), 67.

woman. However, two important facts invalidate such an argument. First, there is no pronouncement of higher status of one gender over another in the narrative (Gen. 2). Secondly, the man and woman are *created*, not *birthed as siblings*, and therefore they occupy a different category—one that stands outside the parameters of primogeniture. In fact, even if the logic of primogeniture is to be applied, many biblical narratives clearly reveal that the primogeniture concept is sometimes disregarded, lost or in some way dysfunctional, so it still is not certain the argument will hold.[17]

There is also a question of whether the man is really created first. For Trible, the argument that man has higher status because he was created sequentially prior to the woman does not hold because, she argues, the first human created is not a man.[18] According to Trible, the first human was sexually undifferentiated and became a man only with the creation of the woman. Trible argues that the term *hā-'ādām*, *'ādām* preceded by the definite article *hā*, signifies "neither a particular person nor the typical person but the creature from the earth—the earth creature." Furthermore, with no physical features mentioned other than nostrils, this creature is not identified sexually.[19] While Trible is indeed right that the term *hā-'ādām* or *'ādām* can identify common humankind rather than particular genders, and that grammatical masculine gender does not necessarily make a noun sexually male, there is no evidence that the body of this first human was not that of a man. In addition, there is no evidence that the first human took the form of a male body upon the creation of the woman. I have no problem in seeing the first human taking the form of a male body. More importantly, even if the first human happens to be undefined sexually, and even if some unmentioned physical transformation that would correspond to the widely accepted principles of gender identification based on the configuration of human genitals did take place, the situation is left unchanged—the first human continues to be identified as man, and the second human continues to be identified as woman. What is more compelling is that the text nowhere mentions or implies hierarchy between the two humans nor associates any sort of ranking within the creation order.

---

17. For instance, firstborn Cain got cursed by God (Gen. 4:1-16); Isaac was chosen, even though Ishmael was Abraham's firstborn (Gen. 16:15; 17:19-22); Esau "lost" his firstborn privileges to his younger brother Jacob (Gen. 25:23; 27); Joseph prevailed over firstborn Reuben (Gen. 48:22-26; cf. 1 Chron. 5:1-2), as did the younger Ephraim over Manasseh (Gen. 48:12-20). For more references related to the failure of primogeniture, see Webb, *Slaves, Women & Homosexuals*, 136–8.
18. Trible, *God and the Rhetoric of Sexuality*, 80, 97.
19. Ibid., 80.

The argument for women's subjugation being based on the "fact" that the first woman was created from the first man also does not hold, as we shall see. Genesis 2:21-22 says that YHWH God put the first human into a deep sleep, took a part from the first human body, and from this built a woman. The identification of the body part that God takes, ṣēlâ, despite the common translation as "rib," is actually unclear.[20] In other parts of the Old Testament, the term represents sides or leaves of architectural structures such as a door, the tabernacle, the ark of the covenant, the altar (Exod. 25:12; 26:26, 27; 36:25, 31, 32; 37:3, 5; 38:7; 1 Kgs 6:34), the side chambers of the temple (1 Kgs 6:5, 6; Ezek. 41:5, 6, 26), the planks or boards of the temple wall (1 Kgs 6:15, 16), or sometimes even the side of a hill (2 Sam. 16:13). So, while the use of the term in other parts of the Bible does not clarify which human body part is in view in Genesis 2, the fact that a part of the first human body serves as the essential ingredient used in the creation of the second tallies well with the concepts of sameness and proximity evoked by the phrase 'ēzer kĕnegdô. Thus, while it may not be possible to solve what body part ṣēla' is exactly, the sharing of flesh, bone or whatever it might be implies that the two human beings will form a pair or partnership, one founded on sameness. The woman and the man are composed of the same material and are partners. Therefore, the creation of woman from man as the "helper like his self" ('ēzer kĕnegdô) primarily manifests sameness and togetherness rather than subjugation of one over the other. This sameness and togetherness is acknowledged by the man when he meets the woman.

Meeting of the Man and the Woman (Genesis 2:23-24)

When God brings the woman to the man, he exclaims: "This one at last (is) bone of my bones and flesh of my flesh; this one will be called woman, for from man this one was taken" (Gen. 2:23). The deep connection and sameness between the man and the woman are substantively established in the man's expression.

Bone of My Bones and Flesh of My Flesh
The expression "bone of my bones, flesh of my flesh" reflects kinship. For instance, in Gen. 29:14 Laban says of his nephew Jacob: "my bone

---

20. Though this term is traditionally translated as "rib," that the term is unclear has been widely noted. See, for instance, Karalina Matskevich, *Construction of Gender and Identity in Genesis: The Subject and the Other* (New York: T&T Clark, 2019), 18–19; Zevit, *What Really Happened?*, 138–50.

and flesh"; in Gen. 37:27 Judah tells his brothers that since Joseph is their own "flesh" they are not to lay hands on him; in 2 Sam. 5:1 the tribes of Israel say to David, "we are your bone and your flesh"; in 2 Sam. 19:13 David says to priests Zadok and Abiathar, "you are my bone and my flesh." Therefore, in Genesis 2, in exclaiming that the woman is his bone and flesh, the man is pronouncing sameness and togetherness in the sense of belonging together in kinship; this comes without any nuance of subordination being expressed. To belong to one kinship group means to share the same blood lineage, to be together in a group. The Paite Zomi tribe also has a similar expression, *I mi I sa*, which literally translates "our people, our flesh"; this is a term used to refer to members of the same tribe or people. The expression connotes, as does the Hebrew phrase "bone of my bones, flesh of my flesh," belongingness, sameness, togetherness and connectedness between kinship members and within tribe(s).

The expression *zōʾt hapaʿam*, "this time, at last, finally" (Gen. 2:23), reinforces sameness as it reveals how the human could not relate or identify fully and wholly with any other being except for the woman who is created *like* him, sharing the same humanity.[21] Thus the expression "bone of my bones, flesh of my flesh" of the man emphasizes fulfilment in sameness and togetherness rather than of differentiation or hierarchical distinction between the first man and the woman. As well as being made from the same material, their names also co-relate, as the following analysis will illustrate.

The Man Names the Woman
Having identified the woman as bone of his bones and flesh of his flesh, the man calls her woman, *'iššâ*, because out of man, *'îš*, she was taken (Gen. 2:23b). This naming of the woman by the man can easily be interpreted as subordination. However, the word-play in the Hebrew between *'îš* ("man") and *'iššâ* ("woman") indicates their connection, rather than subjugation. In fact, the woman is already referred to as *'iššâ* in Gen. 2:22, the verse before the naming (2:23). In contrast to God bringing the animals and birds to the human to see what he will name them (2:19-20), the woman is already "named" and simply brought to the first human so that the human pair can be together. In bringing her to the man, YHWH God wants him to recognize her and accept her reality.[22] Furthermore,

---

21. Michelle Lee-Barnewall, *Neither Complementarian nor Egalitarian: A Kingdom Corrective to the Evangelical Gender Debate* (Grand Rapids: Baker Academic, 2016), 136.

22. Matskevich, *Construction of Gender and Identity in Genesis*, 20.

even in naming the animals, nothing is said of that naming role to suggest a domination over the animals (Gen. 2:20).

A study of naming events in the Old Testament will help us see whether there is a dominating aspect related to naming. One common trait in naming events of the Old Testament is that names are given meaningfully, mostly describing the name bearer or the situations around the birth. For instance, in Gen. 3:20, the man named his wife "Eve" because she was the mother of all living things, implying the essence of the name-bearer. Eve did not become the mother of all living things because of her name but, rather, she was named so as to reflect what she was. Similarly, Esau is named after the trait he already possessed—being red and hairy (Gen. 25:25). Many names derive from the situation the parents found themselves to be in around the time of the birth of the child. For instance, the name Ishmael, meaning "God will hear," reflects how YHWH heard the mother Hagar in her difficult situation of carrying her child (Gen. 16:11). Other similar examples can be seen in how Lamech named his son Noah (Gen. 5:28-29), how Leah named her sons (Gen. 29:32, 33, 34, 35; 30:11, 13, 18, 20), Rachel naming her sons (Gen. 30:6, 8), Tamar naming her sons (Gen. 38:29, 30), and Joseph naming his sons (Gen. 41:51, 52). These namings are reflective of the situations around the births and create meaningful connections between the namers and named. As Ramsey asserts, these namings of children do not indicate parental supremacy or control but are rather the rightful duty of the parents.[23]

That naming does not indicate superiority is undeniably seen in the event of Hagar's naming of the divine. Hagar, a slave-woman sent away from her master's house, named the divine who spoke to her as "El-roi" (Gen. 16:13). Here, clearly, the divine is not subordinate to Hagar, and does not become so by Hagar's naming. Instead of indicating authority over the named, Hagar's naming reflects a connection between the namer Hagar and the named divine, rather than an exercising of authority.

Certainly, some naming events do suggest control or subordination, such as naming of places by conquerors and re-naming of subjects by kings. For example, in Deut. 3:14 a place is named after its conqueror; in Josh. 19:47 and Judg. 18:29 a city is named after the inhabitants' ancestor's name; and in 1 Kgs 16:24 a place is named after its owner. However, these namings are just different contexts. In a few other instances, a foreign king renames subjects, and that may imply control or subordination—such as when Joseph is given a new name by Pharaoh in Gen. 41:45

---

23. George W. Ramsey, "Is Name-Giving an Act of Domination in Gen. 2:23 and Elsewhere?," *CBQ* 50 (1988): 32.

(other similar cases are in 2 Kgs 23:34; 24:17). Yet, even such cases, as Ramsey rightly notes, cannot be generalized nor be directly utilized to suggest subordination in the naming of the woman in Gen. 2:23.[24] Such an implication of subordination from the naming of conquered places or captured subjects does not suggest subordination in the naming of the woman in Gen. 2:23, because the namer here, the man, did not create, conquer or own the named, the woman. This survey of naming in the Old Testament shows that there is no evidence for inherent authority of the namer over the named.[25] There is no reason to suggest the man's naming of the woman as indicative of his authority or higher status over her.

A similar concept of connectedness is seen in the naming tradition of the Paite tribe. The Paite tribe has a unique naming tradition: babies are not named by their parents, and names are not arbitrarily given; instead, naming is governed by kinship, with grandparents being the ones to name their grandchildren.[26] The deep connection between the namer and the named is best seen in how the name is constructed. In the Paite culture, the last word or syllable of the namer's name should be the first part of the named baby. For example, *Chingkhongai* may name her granddaughter *Ngaimuanching*. Normally, a special bond or relationship develops between the namer and the named. For example, a namer blesses his/her named through prayers and/or gifts and also the named honors his/her namer by giving gifts and such. There are also specific terminologies for a named to address his/her namer, *tappa* (male) or *tapnu* (female), and a namer to his/her named, *minsakpa* (male) or *minsaknu* (female). It is also very common in the Paite community to compare a child or person with the looks or character of his/her namer; for instance, *A tappa/tapnu a sun a pil eive*, meaning, "He/she is wise because he/she takes after his/her namer." Furthermore, as in the naming events of the Old Testament, many Paite names are given to reflect the situation of the child or family,

---

24. Ibid.

25. For a complete list of actual naming events in the Old Testament, see Andrew F. Key, "The Giving of Proper Names in the Old Testament," *JBL* 83 no. 1 (1964): 55–9.

26. In the naming system of the Paite tribe, the firstborn is named by the paternal grandparents—the grandfather names a baby boy and the grandmother names a baby girl. Maternal grandmothers name the second or later baby girl. If the firstborn child is a daughter, the paternal grandmother supplies the name; if the second child is a son, the paternal grandfather names the boy. From the third child on, paternal uncles or aunties name their nephews or nieces. So, by tradition the maternal side gets to name just one child, a girl child, and the rest of the children are named by the paternal family side.

and since becoming Christians, many names ascribe God's character or God's blessings.

Naming concepts of the Hebrew Bible and Paite tribal culture today share commonality in that naming conveys the special relation between namer and named. Such a connection seems to be the case as well in the naming of the woman (*'iššâ*) by the man (*'iš*) in Gen. 2:23b, rather than establishing supremacy or superiority. The theme of togetherness between the man and the woman is further established by the narrator in the next verse (Gen. 2:24).

A Man Shall Cling to His Wife
The speech of the man in Gen. 2:23 is followed by the narrator's statement: "Therefore, a man shall leave his father and mother and cling to his wife and they shall be one flesh" (Gen. 2:24). "Therefore" here continues the theme of sameness seen in the previous verse—"bone of bones and flesh of flesh"—with the statement that the man will cling to his wife and become one flesh. Instead of establishing a hierarchy between the man and woman, the narrator treats them together, and stresses their togetherness by treating them as a separate unit from his parents.

The term for "cling," *dābāq*, implies affection, loyalty or staying together. For instance, in Gen. 34:3, Shechem's heart is drawn to Dinah; in 1 Kgs 11:2, Solomon holds fast to his foreign wives; in Ruth 1:14, Ruth clings to her mother-in-law; in 2 Sam. 20:2, Judahites stay loyal to David when the Israelites followed Sheba; in 2 Sam. 23:10, David's soldiers stand firm with him and fight the Philistines even after others withdrew. Noteworthy in Gen. 2:24 is how the man and his wife are now seen as a single entity, one differentiated from, and perhaps contrasted to, his parents: the man leaves his father and mother and clings to his wife.[27] Recall earlier also that the man and the woman are seen together as distinct from other works of creation, such as the animals (Gen. 2:20).

The expression "they shall become one flesh" signifies a kinship relation in the ancient Israel context, although the expression also connotes

---

27. Zevit argues that the root of the verb for "leave," *'-z-b*, in some instances rather means "help, repair, fix, make whole," instead of "leave" or "abandon" (Exod. 23:5; Neh. 3:8, 34). As such, in Gen. 2:24, it may make more sense to translate along the lines of the man "supporting" his father and mother while "clinging" to his wife, rather than "leaving" his father and mother. Translating as "support" aligns with the cultural obligation of an Israelite son to care for his parents. Zevit, *What Really Happened*, 156–7. This argument makes sense, yet the point of this verse is more of the one-ness or togetherness of the man with his wife, which is made even more clear and emphasized by its differentiation from his relationship with the parents.

the basic meaning of sexual union between the husband and the wife.[28] That is, the man and woman form unity and relatedness similar to the expression "bone of my bones and flesh of my flesh" in the previous verse (Gen. 2:23). Thus, consistent with the larger narrative, sameness or togetherness, pairness and partnership are the focus in the relationship of the man and the woman. In the Paite tribal concept also, as the dual meaning of becoming "one flesh" signifies, sexual union and marriage are considered to be mutually inclusive, with the formation of a new kinship unit coming about and being confirmed by the bearing of children. Also, while the family of the firstborn son stays home to care for his parents, thereby ensuring generational support and the maintenance of the family lineage, any younger sons move out (*intuan*), marrying and forming new family units. Each married couple has their own family council (*inndongta*), made up of relatives from both the man and woman's side.

Conclusion

This chapter re-examines whether Genesis 2 contains direct support for the institutional subordination of women in the creation narrative of the first man and woman, something that is often claimed by cultures such as the Paite Christian tribe. A literary analysis of Genesis 2 has demonstrated that the overarching message of the narrative in regard to the man and woman is one of sameness and togetherness; there appears to be no hint of any hierarchical ordering between the two. It has been observed that the term often used to argue for the subjugation of women, "helper," can actually be used to refer to someone of a higher status, such as God or king, who offers assistance. In fact, in the majority of cases the term "helper" is used in reference to assistance rendered by a figure of higher status (without any loss of such status); there are considerably fewer instances of low(er) status figures appearing as "helpers." As such, subordinating women from the argument of being created to be "helpers" for men does not hold.

Other terms and phrases often quoted from Genesis 2 to argue for women's subordination were also shown to be not subjugating when read within their own contexts. The "fact" that woman was created *after* man and *from* man, as well as the "fact" that it is the man who names the woman, were shown to be flawed arguments offering no support of an hierarchical distinction between the two sexes. The woman being created from man manifests that both are of the same material, and the naming

---

28. Wenham, *Genesis*, 71.

implies a deep connection between the namer and the named. Therefore, such logic substantiates and exhibits the deep connection, sameness and togetherness between the man and the woman. In sum, what is emphasized in the biblical text is the sameness and togetherness of the first two human beings, who are treated together as partners or as a pair. We now turn to examine the relationship between man and woman in Genesis 3, which continues the consistent theme of sameness and togetherness evident in Genesis 1 and 2.

Chapter 5

FIRST MAN AND WOMAN TOGETHER IN THE GARDEN (GENESIS 3)

Introduction

Genesis 3 is perhaps the most cited biblical text to argue for women's subordination. An example that stands out is Gen. 3:16b, which states: "And he shall rule you (the woman)." This utterance from God has been readily and amply used by many, including Paite Christians, to argue for women's subordination and male's authority over female as God-willed and biblical. But, is the ultimate authority of males and the subjugation of women actually what the narrative of Genesis 3 institutes? In addition to the statement about man ruling over woman (Gen. 3:16), other negative stereotypes of women are also drawn from the narrative of Genesis 3, such as: women being easily deceived and, upon usurping men's place of authority, instrumental in leading men into sin (Gen. 3:3, 6); women being the cause of fatal trouble when obeyed by men/husbands (Gen. 3:17-19). Yet are these interpretive inferences actually established in the narrative of Genesis 3? Should they be taken to be the biblical/Christian law or guide on gender order? To be faithful to the biblical message, which is the sincere desire of a Christian society like the Paite tribe, it is essential to study these terms and statements within their own contexts in the narrative of Genesis 3 before implementing them today as *the* biblical law or order.

In this chapter, several elements of Genesis 3 that have been used to promulgate women's subjugation as biblical will be re-examined. As will be elaborated below, a close analysis of the biblical text demonstrates that terms and phrases appearing in Genesis 3 are rather ambiguous and not inherently subordinating of one gender. Interestingly, we have here a situation somewhat similar to the ambiguity surrounding the term "helper" in Genesis 2 whereby the infamous term "rule" in Gen. 3:16b is somewhat opaque, with two alternative meanings possible—"rule" or "like, resemble". Also, nowhere in the text of Genesis 3 is the woman condemned, nor is the man prohibited from listening to the woman, contrary to the tendencies of today's readers to blame the woman. Instead, the theme of the togetherness of the man and woman, already seen in Genesis 1 and 2, continues throughout Genesis 3—in the human couple's mutual violation of God's command, in the shared judgments they receive as well as their continued existence alongside each other after God's pronouncement of judgment has been made.

Man with Woman in Disobeying God's Command (Genesis 3:1-12)

Genesis 3 continues the narrative from the creation of the first man and woman (Gen. 2) into the garden of Eden, with the man, the woman and a serpent as the main characters. The one episode in Genesis 3 which is most often used to defame the woman is the eating of the fruit from the tree that had been expressly forbidden to the human couple by God. The woman's response to the serpent's query about whether they can eat from any tree in the garden (Gen. 3:1) contains the added detail that the human couple are not to touch the tree, let alone eat from it (Gen. 3:2-3)—a detail which is not included in the original command (Gen. 2:16-17). This additional statement by the woman is easily construed as women being talkative and untrustworthy, as being unsuitable bearers or agents of God's commands. However, if the text is read carefully, we can see that the narrative does not indicate where the additional detail comes from, nor how the divine command, which was issued before the creation of the woman, reached her. Therefore, while it is easy to blame the woman for the additional element that appears in her citation of the tree command to the serpent, it is quite possible that it was the man or God—who else was on hand to communicate the pre-existing command to the subsequently formed woman?—who added the "not to touch" component, and that the woman is simply retelling what she had heard. There is just not enough information to know whether the woman changed the command or not. As such, we cannot blame the woman for this additional phrase.

Another statement that has been used to lay blame on the woman is that not only did she eat from the tree, but she also gave some to her man who was with her and he ate (Gen. 3:6). Significantly, Ortlund's argument that it was the woman's usurping of men's headship that was the cause of sin is precisely that used by tribal Christians like the Paite. Ortlund argues that since the text does not say "Her husband, who was with her, also took some and ate it," it carries the effective meaning that "Eve usurped Adam's headship and led the way into sin."[1] It is noteworthy, however, that the text nowhere blames the woman. More significant is that the narrative particularly mentions that the man was "with" (*'im*) the woman. Simply stating that the woman gave the fruit to her husband and he also ate would be enough to communicate how the man got to eat the fruit. But mentioning the seemingly redundant information that the man was *with* the woman shows consistency with the theme of togetherness of the man and woman.

"With" can imply togetherness beyond physical proximity, such as being in agreement in their action of eating. In Hebrew, the preposition *'im* ("with") can also mean loyalty, companionship and fellowship. For example, God will be *with* Abraham in all he does (Gen. 21:22); God will be *with* Moses (Exod. 3:12); Lot went *with* Abram in his journey of leaving his home (Gen. 13:1); Abram went *with* the men from God (Gen. 18:16); and Joshua together *with* all Israel took Achan (Josh. 7:24). In a similar manner, in Gen. 3:6, the statement "the man who was *with* the woman" depicts how the man and woman are together in their action, not only how close they are physically. In addition, the man himself expresses how the woman was given to be "with" him as if in acknowledgment of the purpose of the man and woman as togetherness. When YHWH God questioned the man if he had eaten from the tree of which he was commanded not to, he answered: "The woman whom you gave to be *with* me, she gave me from the tree and I ate" (Gen. 3:12). Interestingly, the man does not say "the man you gave to be my helper" (cf. Gen. 2:18), but rather "the man you gave to be *with* me," indicating the man also understood the woman was given to be *with* him. From a literary point of view, the configuration "you gave to be with me…she gave it to me" in Gen. 3:12 is noteworthy in that while the fruit is simply given to the man, the woman is given to be *with* the man, as Kraus points out.[2] The man and the woman are created to be *with* each other, and the narrative of Genesis 3 treats them together, as a pair and as partners, with no subordination of one to the other being promulgated. On account of their eating from the forbidden tree, God lays out judgments upon the woman and the man, ones that, when compared, display observable similarities.

---

1. Ortlund, "Male–Female Equality and Male Headship," 107.
2. Helen Kraus, *Gender Issues in Ancient and Reformation Translations of Genesis 1–4* (Oxford: Oxford University Press, 2011), 30.

Judgment on the Woman (Genesis 3:16)

God's judgment of the woman reads (Gen. 3:16):

> "I will multiply your toil and childbearing;
> In pain you will give birth to children.
> And to your husband will be your desire;
> And he will rule you."

What is noteworthy in this judgment is that, first and foremost, there is no indictment along the lines of "Because you did this...," which is seen in judgments of both the serpent and the man (Gen. 3:14, 17). That is, the biblical text contains no accusation against the woman—no matter how much some modern readers today may want to throw an accusation upon the woman. Some read the first line of the judgment as hendiadys—"toil in childbearing"—meaning that the pain encountered in childbearing will be increased.[3] That is to say that the "toil" is from "childbearing." Others read the "toil" and "childbearing" separately, and therefore childbearing and toil (from other labor) will be increased.[4] That is to say that there is childbearing hardship as well as another kind of toil described in this line. Grammatically, either position is possible. Whether one understands the line as a hendiadys or not, the core theme of the narrative—the similarity of the woman and man—still holds, as can be seen in the components of the judgment.

Pain and Toil for the Woman: Not Unlike the Man's

There are two terms for pain and toil for the woman, *'iṣābôn* and *'eṣeb*. Both terms derive from the same Hebrew root, *'ṣb*, though, importantly, this root is not commonly linked to the pain experienced during childbirth in the Hebrew Bible.[5] The word for pain in the second line, *'eṣeb*—"in pain you will give birth to children"—is not limited to pain from physical labor (Ps. 127:2; Prov. 5:10; 14:23) but also connotes hurts caused psychologically (Prov. 15:1). Therefore, the use of this term, an unusual and not technical term for labor pain, acknowledges the pain of woman beyond physical pain, encompassing all forms of hurt and distress—physical, emotional, psychological—that come with bringing a child into the world.

---

3. For example, Sarna, *Genesis*, 27; Wenham, *Genesis*, 81.
4. For example, Carol Meyers, *Rediscovering Eve: Ancient Israelite Women in Context* (Oxford: Oxford University Press, 2013), 89–90.
5. Common terms for "pain" in childbearing include *ḥul* (Isa. 26:17, 18; 45:10; Mic. 4:10; Jer. 4:31; 6:24), *ḥēbel* (Isa. 13:8), and *ṣîr* (Isa. 21:3).

The word for toil in the first line, *'iṣābôn*, is the same term used for the toil that the man will suffer to get food from the ground (Gen. 3:17). Therefore, some argue that the woman and man might not have been assigned totally different roles. For instance, Meyers interprets the term *'iṣābôn* and thereby the first part of Gen. 3:16 as a reference to the increased physicality of the woman's contribution to the society through her productive work—and not pregnancy, which is expressed in the second part.[6] Hess also argues that the term in the context of the garden of Eden indicates that the woman was to work side-by-side with the man in tilling the land.[7] This line of understanding makes sense since in Gen. 5:29, the only other place where the same term is used, it is in reference to agricultural work. Yet, the immediate context of Gen. 3:16 mentions only childbearing and childbirthing, which are unique to women. So, it is difficult not to see the term *'iṣābôn* as referring and amplifying the toil of childbearing. What is clear, however, from the use of the same term is that the woman's toil is considered as the same level of toil of the man (Gen. 3:17), though it is unclear whether the woman is to be performing the same tasks as the man. The pain and toil of the woman is seen as no less important or intense but rather the same as the man's.

Desire for Man and Man's Rule
The second part of the judgment towards the woman, which is often used to subordinate women, may be the only overtly subordinating one in Genesis 1–3. In light of this, a re-examination of the statement is essential. Genesis 3:16b states, "to your husband will be your desire; and he will rule you." The term for "desire," *tĕšûqâ*, appears three times in the Old Testament—in Gen. 3:16, in Gen. 4:7 and in Song 7:11. Here in Gen. 3:16 it is generally understood in one of three ways. One interpretation views the "desire" in terms of competing or even adversarial struggles for control, will, status or equality, or power between the woman and the man.[8] This way of understanding mostly derives from comparing it with

---

6. Carol L. Meyers, "Gender Roles and Genesis 3:16 Revisited," in *A Feminist Companion to Genesis*, ed. Athalya Brenner (Sheffield: Sheffield Academic Press, 1993), 131.

7. Richard S. Hess, "Equality With and Without Innocence," in *Discovering Biblical Equality: Complementarity Without Hierarchy*, ed. Ronald W. Pierce and Rebecca Merrill Groothuis, 2nd ed. (Downers Grove: IVP Academic, 2005), 91.

8. For example, Susan T. Foh, "What is the Woman's Desire," *WTJ* 37 (1975): 376–83; Walter Vogels, "The Power Struggle Between Man and Woman (Gen. 3:16b)," *Bib* 77 (1996): 206; Hess, "Equality With and Without Innocence," 93; Trible, *God and the Rhetoric of Sexuality*, 128. Some interpret it as a power struggle

Gen. 4:7, which expresses that while sin will "desire" Cain, he has to "rule" over it. The term in Gen. 3:16 can indeed be construed as "desire for power," as in Gen. 4:7, particularly as both "desire" and "rule" are used in either references. The problem, however, is that in Gen. 4:7 the struggle is between a man and an abstract sin, while in Gen. 3:16 it is between two humans. A second understanding associates the term *těšûqâ* with sexual desire, drawing a connection with childbearing mentioned earlier in the verse and also by comparing with Song 7:11, which has romantic overtones between a male and a female lover.[9] A third way of understanding the term is to read *těšûqâ* as "returning," that is, the woman *returns* to her husband. This understanding mainly derives from two reasonings—one, from a secondary development of the root of the term,[10] and second, following translation of the term as "returning" in ancient versions and translations (such as LXX).[11] Understanding the exact meaning of the term remains a puzzle. For instance, after claiming that *těšûqâ* "has clear sexual connotations," Kraus quickly adds, "(apart

caused by woman's usurping of headship earlier: "Because she usurped his headship in the temptation, God hands her over to the misery of competition with her rightful head. This is justice, a measure-for-measure response to her sin." Ortlund, "Male–Female Equality," 109.

9. Such as, among others, Wenham, *Genesis*, 81; Fretheim, *Genesis*, 363.

10. Zevit argues for understanding *těšûqâ* from a secondary development of the root *š-q-q* which includes a psychological aspect/realm rather than just physical (Isa. 29:8; Ps. 107:9). Following that, the word in Gen. 3:16 will be "a desire or longing of the woman to be with her man/husband." Zevit, *What Really Happened?*, 210.

11. Lohr finds that in most ancient versions and translations (such as LXX, *Jubilees*, Old Latin, OT Peshitta, some Targums) the word *těšûqâ* is rendered as "return" or "turning" rather than "desire." The LXX uses *apostrophe*, a term that indicates a return or a turning, while Greek has terms that would express the sense of "desire" or "craving" such as *epithumia* (used in Gen. 31:30) or *hormē*. The Old Latin uses *conversio* in Gen. 3:16 (as well in Gen. 4:7 and Song 7:11). The Peshitta also uses a term for "return," and in the Targums, *Onqelos* uses *tywbh*, which means "turning," "repentance" or "response." Lohr also examines the seven appearances of the term in non-biblical texts from Qumran and contends that in all of its appearances translating the term as "return" fits and in most cases is more appropriate than rendering it as "desire." Joel N. Lohr, "Sexual Desire? Eve, Genesis 3:16 and תשוקה," *JBL* 130 no. 2 (2011): 227–46.

Macintosh also comes to a similar conclusion as Lohr after examining the term through comparative philology and its usage in ancient versions such as LXX, Latin, Peshitta and such, in addition to the three references in the Hebrew Old Testament and seven references in the Dead Sea Scrolls—that the meaning of the term is not physical desire but more of concern, preoccupation and (single-minded) devotion. A. A. Macintosh, "The Meaning of the Hebrew תשוקה," *JSS* 61, no. 2 (2016): 365–87.

from the sin that is waiting to possess Cain in the rather problematic verse 4:7); its only other occurrence is in the Song of Songs (7:10[11]), where the context is clearly erotic."[12] Given the inconclusive nature of defining the term from other occurrences, a re-examination of the term within its immediate context is imperative.

The pronouncement upon the woman does not introduce an entirely new situation for her.[13] The judgment is not that the woman will *now* bear children, but simply that the pain associated with it will be increased. That is, that pain is experienced during childbirth is not something new, the result of the divine judgment; instead, God is now increasing what seems to have been already present. In that sense, the "desire for your man" is referring to how her purpose for being created—to be "with" the man—is intensified. There are instances where togetherness or being "with" each other is mentioned in regard to the man. For instance, in Gen. 3:6 the man is said to be "with" the woman; in 3:12 the man expressed the woman as put to be "with" him; and in 2:24 the man is said to cling to the woman. On the other hand, there is no such meaningful mention or instance from the woman's side. Thus, it is possible that the "desire" in this judgment speech is about intensifying the woman's purpose to be "with" the man. The sense of "desire," then, while it could include a sexual tone, would also encompass the whole realm of human need to be *with* another human being, which other creations such as animals were unable to fulfill (Gen. 2:19-20).[14] The second part of the sentence, however, seems to create some tension for the desire to be together.

"Man will Rule *Woman" or "Man will* be Like *Woman"? (Genesis 3:16b)*

The second part of the judgment, which reads "and he will rule you," is frequently used to legitimate women's subordination. As Meyers succinctly explains, "Perhaps more than any other text in the Hebrew Bible, this line has been used to justify gender hierarchy: divinely

---

12. Kraus, *Gender Issues in Ancient and Reformation*, 33. Cassuto considered Gen. 4:7 to be "one of the most difficult and obscure" sentences in the Bible. U. Cassuto, *A Commentary on the Book of Genesis*, trans. Israel Abrahams (Jerusalem: Magnes, 1972), 1:208.

13. Zevit, *What Really Happened?*, 211.

14. Condren also comes to a similar conclusion, understanding this term as belongingness or togetherness. He bases his conclusion on the observation that the term *těšûqâ* has quite consistently been understood to mean "returning" in ancient versions, as well as on a consideration of the relatedness of man and woman in the larger context of Gen. 2:18-25. Janson C. Condren, "Toward a Purge of the Battle of the Sexes and 'Return' for the Original Meaning of Genesis 3:16b," *JETS* 60, no. 2 (2017): 227–45.

ordained female subservience and male dominance in all aspects of life."[15] Particularly in the case of the Paite Christian tribe, this line gives male authority such that the male of the family or society should always have the final word, and while girls and women can offer ideas, they should be content with whatever the last word of the man will be. While part of such male dominance is certainly derived from the prevailing patriarchal culture, it also seems to some extent to come from, or to receive confirmation via, Bible translations such as those used by the Paite.

An older translation, one particularly liked and most often used by older generations of Paite Christians, translates the Hebrew of Gen. 3:16b as *aman na tungah thu a nei gige ding*, which renders into English as "he will always (*gige*) have power over you." This translation has "always" added to God's statement, implying it to be like a stipulation or an unchangeable condition or fact determined from the beginning which the woman simply has to accept. Another version (2004) states, *aman nang hon uk ding*, "he will rule you," where the term *uk* has the connotation of authoritative rule, even kingly rule, which gives supreme power to man/husband and implies a subject position for the woman. Like all other biblical texts that have been discussed in the present work, this line from Genesis needs to be understood within its context before using it as an absolute mandate. First, it is necessary to understand the term "rule" in the Hebrew version.

A study of the term for "rule," Hebrew *māšal*, reveals that it has a wide range of usages. Importantly, like the term "helper" seen earlier in Genesis 2, *māšal* is not inherently a term connoting subjugation. The term *māšal* has two possible meanings, "to rule" and "to be like." While the term is commonly translated as "rule," it is important to consider the other meaning of the term. In one important resource used by scholars and translators of the Hebrew Bible, Brown, Driver and Briggs' *A Hebrew and English Lexicon of the Old Testament* (BDB), the term is translated as "represent, be like" in its verbal form. For the nominal meanings, BDB offers two possibilities: "likeness, one like" and "rule, have dominion, reign."[16] Holladay's *Concise Hebrew and Aramaic Dictionary* has "to be equal, become the same, become like something, to compare with" under the derived stems of *māšal*.[17] In Botterweck and Ringgren's *Theological Dictionary of the Old Testament* (*TDOT*) it is judged that the original

---

15. Meyers, *Rediscovering Eve*, 95.

16. BDB lists one more root which means "proverb, parable" in noun form and "use a proverb, speak in parables or sentences of poetry" in verbal form. BDB, 605.

17. William Lee Holladay, *A Concise Hebrew and Aramaic Lexicon of the Old Testament: Based upon the Lexical Work of Ludwig Koehler and Walter Baumgartner* (Grand Rapids: Eerdmans, 1971), 647.

meaning of the verb *māšal* was "be like," with the word now being preserved only in the derived stems (*Niphal, Hiphil, Hithpael*), and the derivative *mōšel* meaning "equal."[18] In Clines' *Dictionary of Classical Hebrew* (*DCH*), two possibilities are given for translating the term in Gen. 3:16—either as "…and/but he will rule over you" or "…and/but he will be like you."[19] Noting that in Gen. 3:16 *māšal* is in *Qal* impf. 3ms form (*yimšāl*), and working with *TDOT*'s observation that the understanding of *māšal* as "be like" is preserved only in derived stems, one could maintain that the meaning of the term appearing in Gen. 3:16b has to be "to rule." However, upon close consideration, two possibilities arise. First, it is possible that the term is actually in the derived *Niphal* form, since it would still possess the same consonantal arrangement as the *Qal* in the unvocalized version of the Hebrew text, as Schmitt points out.[20] Second, it is still possible that Gen. 3:16 is an exception where *māšal* in the *Qal* still means "be like"—and indeed, exceptions to grammatical rules are not uncommon. Therefore, either "to rule" or "to be like" should be considered as equal candidates for translation of *māšal* in Gen. 3:16.

Otwell points out that in Gen. 3:16 "to liken" makes more sense because the preposition (*bĕ*), which governs the object in this verse, makes it more difficult to translate *māšal* as "to rule."[21] He also notes that "to rule" came to be adopted only from the time of the Septuagint, from about 200 BCE.[22] In that same vein, Schmitt argues for the "like" meaning of *mšl* in Gen. 3:16 by considering the similarity between the man and woman in Genesis 2–3, as well as how husbands are not set as rulers over their wives in other parts of Genesis.[23] He further presents other examples, such as Joel 2:17, Job 41:25 (41:33 Eng.), and 2 Sam. 23:3,

---

18. In derived forms to mean "be like" or "resemble" the terms appears in Isa. 14:10 (*Niphal*), Job 30:19 (*Hithpael*), Pss. 28:1; 49:13, 21 (*Niphal*), Isa. 46:5 (*Hiphil*). See K.-M. Beyse, "*māšal* I," *TDOT* 9:65.

19. *DCH* 5:531, 533, 537.

20. The *n* prefix of the *Niphal* form would assimilate and have the same form as *Qal* (*ymšl*). John J. Schmitt, "Like Eve, Like Adam: *mšl* in Gen. 3,16," *Bib* 72 no. 1 (1991): 16 n. 52.

21. Otwell, however, eventually dismisses translating it as "to liken" because he reasons that in order to have the meaning of "to liken" it has to have an *n* prefixed to the root, that is, be in the *Niphal* form. Schmitt rightly responds to Otwell that even had it been a *Niphal* stem, the *n* would assimilate and thus the consonantal reading would still be identical to the *Qal* stem as we have it now in Gen. 3:16 (*ymšl*). Ibid.

22. Beyond noting this in a footnote, Otwell does not discuss further. John H. Otwell, *And Sarah Laughed: The Status of Woman in the Old Testament* (Philadelphia: Westminster Press, 1977), 197–8 n. 15.

23. Schmitt, "Like Eve, Like Adam," 1–22.

that reveal ambiguities in translating *māšal* either as "rule" or "like" and where ancient translations and versions rendered different meanings from modern translations.[24] Thus, Schmitt convincingly argues that as in these three instances the same term *mšl b-* in Gen. 3:16 is open to ambiguity, even though most have taken for granted the meaning "rule."

To understand the term *māšal* in Gen. 3:16, it is crucial to examine its immediate context. In Gen. 3:14-19, the unit about God's judgment on the three characters—the serpent, the woman and the man—some tensions are observable among the characters. The relationship between the man and the ground, which mentions no struggle earlier (Gen. 2:15), is now put in tension as the man has to work the ground harder to earn his livelihood (Gen. 3:17, 19). The judgment on the serpent also pronounces enmity between the serpent and the woman and their respective descendants (Gen. 3:15). That is, while there was no mention of such enmity between them earlier in the narrative, there is now tension between the woman and the serpent. Reading in line with the tension that develops in the other two characters, tension also develops between the man and the woman. In the immediate context, then, reading the term *māšal* as "to rule" makes more sense than "to resemble." There is no mention of struggles earlier in the togetherness of the man and the woman. There is no mention of desire earlier either, but now the text states that her desire is to be with her man and he will rule her (Gen. 3:16). In other words, while togetherness between the man and the woman seems to have been the natural state of affairs earlier, now they have to make an effort to achieve and preserve it. Just as the man has to exert himself in order to work the ground, so too the togetherness between the man and woman, though not lost, requires sustained effort.

It is significant to note from the judgment of the woman that the togetherness of the human couple is not lost. And nor does the statement establish the man as ruler over the woman—though the words are often misinterpreted. For instance, Ortlund confers male domination with this

24. Ibid., 10–11. In Joel 2:17, while most modern translations imply the sense of "make a proverb, to mock" (NRSV and NIV: "a byword among the nations"; TNK: "to be taunted by"; but cf. NKJV: "that the nations should rule over them"), many ancient versions understood the term to mean "to rule" (LXX: "that peoples rule over them"; Vulgate: "that nations rule over them") and there is no indication that they had a different *Vorlage*. In Job 41:25 (41:33 Eng.), where most modern English translations and the LXX understand the term as "be like" (NRSV: "it has no equal"; NIV: "nothing on earth is his equal"; NKJV: "nothing like him"; but cf. TNK: "there is no one on land who can dominate him"), the Targum and the Peshitta opt for the "to rule" meaning. In 2 Sam. 23:3, the LXX has "parable" instead of "rule."

5. First Man and Woman Together in the Garden (Genesis 3) 103

comment: "As the woman competes with the man, the man, for his part, always holds the trump card of male domination to 'put her in her place'."[25] Such an interpretation is akin to that subscribed to by the patriarchal Paite Christian society. Such a reading, however, seems to me to be far-fetched and not at all reflected in the text. If making the man ruler over the woman is the aim of the narrative, it could be done plainly and clearly—as we find elsewhere in the Old Testament. Consider, for example, Est. 1:22 where King Xerxes issues a letter that every man in his kingdom should be ruler over his own household. In that statement the term for "ruler" is not *māšal* but *śārar*, in the participle form. In contrast, the term in Gen. 3:16 is *māšal*, in the imperfect form. The term *śārar*, unlike *māšal*, implies ruling as a chief or head, official or prince with authority. A study of the usage of the term *māšal* ("rule") in other instances will shed more light on how the term does not inherently grant the man a rulership over the woman.

Genesis 1:16-18 is the closest reference where the same term *māšal* is used. In Gen. 1:16-18 the term means "rule" but it includes "an element of service," meaning the greater and lesser lights are to "rule" over the day and the night (also see Ps. 136:8-9).[26] That is, the lights are to illuminate the day and the night, not to control or subjugate them. The term is also used in reference to God as the ruler of Jacob (Ps. 59:14 [59:13 Eng.]) and of all (Pss. 22:29 [22:28 Eng.]; 103:19; 1 Chron. 29:12; 2 Chron. 20:6). It is used for ruling justly (2 Sam. 23:3), as well as with restricted authority, where a master has no right ("rule") to sell his slave woman (Exod. 22:8). The term is also used for self-control of one's own spirit/temper (Prov. 16:32). In other instances, "ruling" can indeed imply domination over those ruled (Deut. 15:6, Israel will "rule" over nations; Judg. 14:4; 15:11, the Philistines dominate Israel). Sometimes it is also used to refer to a king's domination (Josh. 12:5, King Og rules a region; 1 Kgs 5:1 [4:21 Eng.], Solomon rules over kingdoms; Dan. 11:43, the king of the North rules over Egypt). Furthermore, in contrast to another term for "rule," *mlk*, which is commonly associated with king's rule, *mšl* focuses less on the ruler and more on the rule or dominion itself (Gen. 45:8, 26; Josh. 12:2, 5; Judg. 8:22-23; 14:4; 15:11; 2 Chron. 9:26).[27]

As we see in this survey of usages of *māšal* as "to rule" in other instances, the term does not inherently connote authority or absolute rulership. While the term is used at some instances for kings, masters or nations, clearly in Gen. 3:16 the man is not made king nor the woman his subject; the man is not made a master nor the woman his slave.

25. Ortlund, "Male–Female Equality," 109.
26. H. Gross, "*māšal* II," *TDOT* 9:71.
27. Ibid., 69.

Interpreting it that way goes contrary to the context of Genesis 3. As Hess clearly puts it, "It is not a command for one sex to rule over the other any more than Genesis 3:17-19 is a command for all Israelite men to be farmers or a prohibition of the use of weed-killer."[28] More importantly, the main theme of the text, "togetherness" between the man and the woman, is not destroyed or cursed. That is, this judgment on the woman does not totally uproot that togetherness nor establish hierarchical rulership.

The above analysis reveals two crucial things about the term *māšal*. First, as in the case of "helper" seen earlier (Gen. 2:18, 20), *māšal* in Gen. 3:16b is not as straightforward as it seems. The term is open to more than one meaning—"rule" and "resemble." While grammatically both readings are defensible, our consideration of the immediate context has shown "rule" to be the more suitable reading in Gen. 3:16. Nonetheless, our exploration of the term's connotations as "rule" shows that the statement "he will rule you" (3:16b) does not make the man a ruler over the woman. The context of Genesis 3 also nowhere states or implies that. Secondly, the choice of this word may even be intentional in that the dual meaning of "rule" and "resemble" should ring in the background. Considering the main theme of sameness and togetherness present throughout, before and after this statement, even though the man will "rule" the woman, the man is also still "like" the woman.

The theme of togetherness or partnership of the woman and the man, rather than ruling, continues to be seen in the narratives following Genesis 3.[29] The woman, Eve, is the speaker and an active character in the rest of the narratives mentioning the first human couple. For example, Eve, not Adam, names the children she and Adam bore (Gen. 4:1, 25). More significantly, there is no instance of Adam becoming ruler over Eve. Also, the matriarch Sarah does not seem to be "ruled over" by the patriarch Abraham. Instead, Sarah is presented as a confident and independent character who has a voice to her husband, Abraham, who listens to her (Gen. 16:2, 5, 6). God even instructs Abraham to listen to his wife Sarah's voice (Gen. 21:10-12). These instances convey how men or husbands are not established as rulers or final authorities over women or their wives. There is also neither condemnation for nor prohibition of the man listening to the woman in Genesis 3, as is elaborated in the judgment of the man.

---

28. Hess, "Equality With and Without Innocence," 92.
29. Schmitt, "Like Eve, Like Adam," 2–4.

Judgment on the Man (Genesis 3:17-19)

God's judgment of the man begins with "Because you listened to the voice of your wife and ate from the tree which I commanded you not to eat..." (Gen. 3:17a). It is easy to indict Adam for listening to his wife by reading the first clause of the statement in isolation. It is critical, however, to read God's statement in its entirety. I concur with Lee-Barnewall's point that the judgment is concentrated on the man's disobeying of God's command (Gen. 3:19), rather than focusing on how he listened to the woman.[30] If the main problem was listening to the voice of the woman, the consequence would be somehow related back to the woman—for instance, we might expect some instruction about what is to be done with/to the woman. (Notice how the serpent and woman are clearly put in a position of enmity for the former's "causing" of the latter to eat, Gen. 3:13, 15.) Instead, just as God's command was about eating—what could and what should not be eaten (Gen. 2:16-17)—so too the judgment also focuses on eating: the man will eat with painful toil all the days of his life, and by the sweat of his brow he will eat until he returns to the ground (Gen. 3:17, 19). Had the biblical text provided a command about listening to his wife we might rightly and reasonably expect to encounter a judgment saying that the man should not listen to his wife. Yet such is lacking from the Genesis account: the judgment is focused primarily on God's command that is recorded and subsequently disobeyed—the command not to eat from the tree.

It is also noteworthy that in the biblical text the woman, Eve, does not speak to the man, Adam. She simply gives some fruit to her husband and he eats it (Gen. 3:6). Zevit's finding is helpful in understanding the phrasing here. He argues that the Hebrew words typically translated as "listening to the voice of" in Gen. 3:17, *šāma'tā lĕqôl*, do not make use of the usual preposition *bĕ*, a grammatical formulation that would support the interpretation of "listening, obeying or acquiescing." Rather, another preposition, *lĕ*, is used in the phrase, implying a slight difference in meaning. Zevit further demonstrates the difference in meaning by citing some other occurrences of the phrase with the preposition *lĕ*, such as Exod. 4:8-9 (twice) and Jer. 18:19. In these references where the phrase "listening to the voice of" makes use of the preposition *lĕ* (instead of the usual *bĕ*) there is, significantly, no preceding speech recorded—rather, there are silent acts. The phrase "listening to the voice of" in these cases thus seem to refer "to acting or evaluating a situation on the basis of an

---

30. Lee-Barnewall, *Neither Complementarian nor Egalitarian*, 133.

observed action, object or person."[31] On the basis of this, as well as the above-mentioned observation that the woman did not actually speak in the narrative, it is justifiable to conclude that Gen. 3:17a refers to an instance of the man *imitating the woman's action* rather than obeying any enunciated directive she gave. Thus, in saying "because you listened to the voice of your wife and ate from the tree which I commanded you not to eat...," God's concern is the fact that he (also) ate from the tree, an act that disobeyed a divine command that was expressly stated in the biblical text (Gen. 2:9).

Another important point in the judgment of the man is its similarity to the woman's. Neither the woman nor the man was cursed—only the serpent and the ground were cursed. Also, while the woman is not accused or indicted and the man is indicted ("Because you..."), similarities still abound in their judgments. As in the case of the woman, whose childbirthing pain is increased rather than newly initiated, there is no completely new condition pronounced in God's judgment of the man. The man's God-ordained tilling of the ground (Gen. 2:5, 15) continues, only now it becomes more arduous, with thorns and thistles magnifying the pain and intensity (Gen. 3:17). As discussed above, the man and woman are to go through the same kind of toil (*'iṣābôn*).

Conclusion

From the analysis of Genesis 3 we can conclude that the elements of the narrative that have frequently and traditionally been used to authorize women's subordination as biblical are not inherently subordinating. In particular, the often-used argument from Genesis 3 that men are to "rule" women (Gen. 3:16) has been shown to be rather ambiguous. With its two possible meanings of "rule" and "resemble," the sense of the sameness and pairness of the man and woman continues to linger even after the statement is made that man will *māšal* woman. As we have seen, the term for *māšal*, which has so frequently been translated as "rule," does not make the man a ruler over the woman. Instead, the purpose of the

---

31. The phrase appears 16 times in the Hebrew Bible with the preposition *lĕ* (as opposed to 107 times with *bĕ*). Zevit notes that the technical linguistic terminology for such a string, "hear/listen+to/for+sound/voice" is "syntagm." A syntagm is a sequence of individual words that in combination constitute a single unit with its own new meaning (an example in English would be "How do you do?," which is rather a greeting/way of saying "Hello"—the actual meaning of the words involved, especially the meaning of "do," having mostly lost their primary meanings). Zevit, *What Really Happened?* 220–1.

man and woman being *with* each other is emphasized in the text. In the judgments of the woman and the man, too, the human couple continue to be treated the same, together—they will experience the same level of toil. The judgment of the man also does not contain condemnation nor prohibition of the man arising from him listening to his wife. In fact, even in the judgment where tension arises between the man and woman, there is no expression of stipulation for a subjugating hierarchical order of one over another. The theme of sameness and togetherness holds throughout Genesis 3 and even beyond. Thus, a close reading of the text demonstrates that the biblical narrative of creation of the first two humans does not promulgate women's subjugation.

In sum, as in Genesis 1 and 2, the narrative of the first man and woman in the garden of Eden (Gen. 3) views and treats the man and woman together and the same. The theme of togetherness and likeness is seen throughout the narratives of Genesis 1, 2 and 3, and there is no hint of or linguistic allusion to the woman's subjugation. Our analyses of the first three chapters of Genesis have revealed to us the importance of reading biblical texts carefully in their own contexts before applying them to our cultural contexts today. Such analyses also caution us to reflect more deeply before we make our sincere attempts to apply "biblical lessons" to our unique, rich Christian tribal culture today. This subject will be discussed more fully in the following chapter.

Chapter 6

TOWARD A TRIBAL BIBLICAL HERMENEUTIC

Our study of the Northeast Indian tribal communities and the Genesis creation stories has revealed that, rather than advocating the commonly assumed subordinated status of women, the biblical text actually supports the agency of women and provides an affirmation of their equal status. We have also discovered how Christian missionary movements and their biblical readings have rather contributed to women's subjugation. In this concluding chapter, we will deal with two important issues. The first part of this chapter offers a summary of the findings made in the preceding chapters. The second part will be a brief reflection on the broader topic of how we can cultivate a more faithful and responsible reading of the Bible. In the second part I will offer some guidelines that may be useful for producing more conscientious approaches to and readings of the Bible.

The preceding chapters were primarily concerned with two main tasks. The first was to present a brief survey of the Northeast Indian tribal societies in the pre-Christian era and since the advent of colonialism and Christianity, with a focus on the Paite tribe. Our examination of pre-Christian traditional Paite tribal society, as also reflected in many other tribes of Northeast India, uncovered evidence of women's agency and the relatively higher status of females than is usually assumed. There is no doubt that tribal societies like the Paite were, and still are, male-centered and male-dominated patriarchies. Yet, women were not in a completely subjugated condition. Traces of matrilineal practices and women's agency are evidenced in some folktales and some customary practices. With the coming of colonialism, new systems such as individualized landlords and a money-based economy were introduced. Such systems effectively replaced the communitarian traditions of economy, such as communal land ownership and harmonious cooperative labor, and led to the inauguration of profit-seeking, individualized and hierarchical institutions. This development resulted in an increase in male control, on the one hand, and a corresponding confinement of women to homes and domestic roles, on the other. In the new economy, women's contributions came to be deemed less valued, even valueless, and male-dominated institutions became central to the society.

Christian missionary movements in Northeast India also functioned patriarchally. Witnessing this, traditional patriarchal tribal societies found further confirmation that practicing women's subordination was the normal state of affairs. The newly Christianized tribal societies effectively melded the Christian message and patriarchal habits of the missionaries and came to see the subordinated status of women as "biblical," as the Christian way. In effect, while the coming of Christianity brought with it an improvement in education and general living conditions for both men and women, the deep-rooted ideology of women being subordinate to men became further entrenched. Such was perhaps to be expected, since religious institutions are comparatively more rigid in systematically and structurally subjugating women than the larger "secular" societal institutions in general. Strikingly, while tribal women have thrived in their pursuit of professional careers in medicine, education, politics and so on, the exclusion of Paite women from leadership and decision-making positions within the religious structures is particularly jarring. Such a difference in women's situation within and outside the church is due to the tribe's subscription to the concept of women's subordination as being biblically sanctioned/Christian.

The second task undertaken in the preceding chapters was to offer a close re-reading of the biblical narrative of creation in Genesis 1–3. The aim was to engage with the primary text used to support women's subordination as "biblical." As we have seen, the creation story in Genesis 1–3 (especially chs. 2–3) is often used to argue for women's subordination as biblically ordered since the time of creation. A literary analysis of Genesis 1–3 has demonstrated that the overarching thrust of the creation narrative in regard to the man and woman is sameness and togetherness, rather than a hierarchical ordering between the two. In the creation account of Genesis 1, all created objects and beings are each assigned their purpose. Male and female are the same, with both being created in the image and likeness of God (Gen. 1:26-28). No differentiation between them is noted. Together, male and female share the task of "ruling" over other creation. There is no hidden or implied hierarchical ordering in the status and role of the male and female.

Literary analysis of Genesis 2 also verifies that the elements from Genesis 2 that have customarily been used to authorize women's subordination as biblical are not inherently subordinating. The term "helper" can designate one from a higher status, such as God or king. In fact, in most instances the Hebrew term *'ēzer* is used in reference to a helper coming from a higher status. Surprisingly few cases see the helper occupying the lower status, rendering assistance to someone of a higher status. As such, any attempts to subordinate women based on the argument that the first woman was created to be the lowly helper for the man simply do not hold. Other widely promulgated arguments using the Genesis creation narrative were also shown to be founded on flawed interpretation of the text. Rather than supporting a differentiation and ranking of the sexes, our re-reading of the biblical narrative revealed an emphasis on the sameness and connectedness of the man and woman. That the woman was created from part of the man's body signifies that the two are made of the same flesh, that they share the same material or essence. Naming events in the Old Testament were shown to signify a deep connection between the namer and named, without connotations of authority. As such, the man's naming of the woman, rather than suggesting male control and female subservience, is an expression of the couple's bondedness.

Similarly, the elements in Genesis 3 that have been used to argue for women's subordination were shown not to be inherently subjugating. For instance, the term for "rule," *māšal*, in God's statement to the woman, "he will rule you" (Gen. 3:16), is ambiguous. As we saw, *māšal* carries either the meaning of "to rule" and "be like, resemble." And even though our analysis of the text concludes that "rule" fits better within the immediate context of the passage, the other meaning, "resemble," seems to be carried as well. The sense of the sameness and partnership of the man and woman continues in the narrative even after the statement that "he will rule you." The use of *māšal* in Gen. 3:16 does not make men rulers over women. God's judgments on the woman and man are strikingly similar. For example, the same terms are used and the same level of pain and toil are implied for both the woman and man. Thus, a close re-reading of the biblical text demonstrates that the biblical narrative of the creation of the first two humans does not promulgate women's subjugation. In short, in Genesis 1 the male and female are united in being both created in the same image and likeness of God, together given the same purpose. And the sameness and togetherness of the male/man and female/woman carry throughout Genesis 2 and 3, and beyond. When not read closely and not analyzed carefully, the emphasis of the text on sameness can be easily missed.

Traditional tribal communities like the Paite have a sincere desire to be biblical ones. In that aspiration, however, it is easy and tempting to find affinities with terms such as "helper" used for the woman and "rule" for the man in the creation story and utilize them to institute women's subordination as biblical. Our analysis of the creation story reminds us that it is easy to interpret our own cultural norms as biblical without prior proper study of the biblical (con)texts. This study has also shown that it was/is relatively easy for tribal communities to accept Western cultural norms embedded in the lives and practices of missionaries and the organization of the missionary movements as biblical and Christian. It is my hope that our re-reading of the creation narrative motivates us to read biblical texts on their own terms, that it prompts us to consider the possibility that perhaps we claim our own cultural norms as biblical because we are familiar with and acclimatized to them. Superficial readings of biblical verses can all too easily align with preconceived expectations, and important details can be readily missed. As such, closer analysis of the text in its own context plays an essential role in ensuring that the biblical text is not understood to be saying and supporting something it is not.

The larger goal of this study is to bring tribal spirituality and culture into meaningful conversations with the biblical narratives. Such meaningful conversations can be achieved through ways of reading that are more faithful to the Scripture in its own context and also meaningfully made alive in our tribal contexts.

The Need for Tribal Hermeneutics

We have noted the similarities shared by biblical ancient Israelites and Northeast Indian tribals, including the Paites today—their customary laws, bride prices, being patrilineal and so on. Importantly, the vast majority of the Bible resources available to Northeast Indian tribals derive from a Western context, containing Western thoughts and approaches. These resources are sincerely appreciated and undoubtedly beneficial. But it also means that upon entry into, and engagement with, biblical stories Northeast Indian tribals are engaging with the biblical text through intermediaries, ones that are culturally distanced from both the ancient Israelites and modern-day tribals. As such, it can be rather confusing at times for tribals to attempt to comprehend a biblical context while making use of methods developed from Western contexts, and then to re-translate them to be meaningful in tribal contexts. For instance, in general, Western ways of thoughts are more abstract and philosophical, while tribal thoughts are more concrete and practically oriented. And sometimes there are gaps between the two approaches and ways of thought. It will be more efficient if we could develop indigenous readings of the Bible from Northeast Indian tribal contexts.

As Angami confirms, while contextual Northeast Indian tribal theology is growing and generating adequate academic materials, "contextual biblical hermeneutics or a tribal approach to biblical interpretation is almost non-existent."[1] Tribal hermeneutics is much needed, particularly when we consider that the majority of Northeast Indian tribal groups have now converted to Christianity since the coming of Western missionaries as early as the 1800s. These tribes uphold the Bible as the core of their now-Christian societies. Several decades ago, Frederick Downs also noted the dire need for tribal women's voices and hermeneutics. Downs, a prominent church historian and scholar of the missionary movement in Northeast India, was himself born and raised in the region by missionary parents. Observing that Christianity in the form(s) in which it was brought to the Northeast reinforced and perhaps even advanced patriarchy among the tribes, Downs exhorts that "women belonging to the Northeast Indian tribes would assess and define their own status within society, not being content to let this responsibility rest entirely with men."[2] Certainly, there is a need for both men and women to work together to bring the Bible to life in the tribal communities of Northeast India.

In fact, Keitzar already alerted us to the need for tribal hermeneutics as early as the 1980s in his article entitled "Tribal Perspective in Biblical Hermeneutics Today," published in the *Indian Journal of Theology*. In this article, Keitzar pioneered an initiative for Northeast Indian tribal hermeneutics (though, sadly, little progress has been made). He notes:

> [The religion of the Northeast Indian tribals] is too superficial. The message of the Gospel has not gone deep into the cultural life of tribal Christianity; it is not rooted firmly in the tribal soil; it is still a *xerox-copy* of American Baptist Christianity, or a *duplicate* of western Presbyterianism, or a *carbon-copy* of the charismatic movement of Pentecostalism, or even a *replica* of Roman Catholicism of pre-Vatican-II. It need not be tribalistic, but it can be tribal. What is needed is a tribal Christianity that is founded on the historic faith of the Christian Church on the one hand, and an indigenous Christianity that is planted deep in the cultural life of the tribal people on the other.[3]

---

1. Zhodi Angami, *Tribals, Empire and God: A Tribal Reading of the Birth of Jesus in Matthew's Gospel* (London: Bloomsbury T&T Clark, 2017), 1–2.

2. This appeal was made in Down's 1994 lecture at the North-Eastern Hill University, Shillong, Meghalaya, India. Downs, *Christian Impact on the Status of Women*, iii.

3. Renthy Keitzar, "Tribal Perspective in Biblical Hermeneutics Today," *IJT* 31, no. 3–4 (1982): 310 (emphasis original).

Resources that are based predominantly on abstract logic and rationalism cannot connect meaningfully to Scripture in the tribal ways of thought. And the Bible that we held dear seems alienated and unable to impact our lives, the lives of all members of our community, at a deep level. As Thanzauva and Hnuni deduce, many of the commonly employed biblical methodologies, though necessary and beneficial to some extent, are inadequate for the tribals.[4] Yet, while Thanzauva and Hnuni contend that historical-critical interpretation attempts either to demythologize or reconstruct pure historical factuality of the Bible, and thus is not very helpful to tribal Christians in their self-understanding or their engagement with the biblical narratives in meaningful ways, I see things differently. Tribal Christians like the Paites accept the stories and historical factuality of the Bible, as well as its "mythic" elements. The folklore and folktale culture of the tribals most surely plays a role in the tribals' ready embrace of the Bible and their internalization of it. As such, a tribal hermeneutic needs to be open to additional elements of the biblical text and its synergies with tribal traditions and cultures. This is not to say that methodologies such as historical-critical method are unhelpful—though it is to say that such methods alone are insufficient.

For practical and community-oriented tribals, a more specific tribal hermeneutic would be an essential addition to the basic biblical methodologies. Other methods, such as dialogical hermeneutics, which attempts to re-read biblical materials among other scriptures (of Hindus, Muslim, Buddhist etc.) in light of multi-faith context and in ways applicable in many parts of pluralistic India, do not fit with and meet the specific needs and contexts of the Northeast Indian tribals.[5] For the Christian tribes in Northeast India, whose lives are disconnected with other "mainland" religions and who have already internalized the Bible into their identities, dialogical hermeneutics can lead them away from deeper engagement with the Bible.

I maintain, along with other biblical scholars familiar with Northeast India Christianity, that tribal hermeneutics is a much-needed discipline, one that should work in concert with tribal theology. Indigenous tribal hermeneutics will result in more authentic readings of the Bible into tribal Christian lives, which could thus become more faithfully biblical. Discovering and developing such a hermeneutic is a delicate process, one that needs time and space for careful and deep study. We should not cease to strive for development and continuation of this crucial work.

---

4. Thanzauva and Hnuni, "Ethnicity, Identity and Hermeneutics," 348–51.
5. Ibid., 350.

In order to help the Bible and its stories build meaningful connections to tribal Christian life it is essential that the Bible's life-affirming message is brought out for all members of the communities. A basic first step for that process would be acknowledging and taking seriously two principal tribal values when reading the Bible. First, as practically oriented people who accept and read the Bible as very much part of tribal identity and life, it is vital to consider the lived experience of all community members. Second, it is also important to focus on the interknitted nature of tribal communities.

In reading the Bible as the living Word of God, it is vitally important to study diligently and listen sincerely to what the stories in the Bible are narrating and communicating. It is equally important to take seriously the real, lived experience of all members of our community today. Thanzauva and Hnuni also argue the importance of taking seriously the "day to day struggles for authentic existence" in tribals' reading of the Scripture.[6] When considering the conditions and real experiences of the tribal people, all of its members, including and especially women, should be engaged with. It is important to reflect on how we define our women and how our society nurtures experiences for them that are indeed life affirming. We should consider also whether our patriarchal culture, backed up by our biblical interpretations and theologies, is depriving full dignity and honor to women—who, like men, are created in God's image. As already discussed in the preceding chapters, our present-day society provides ample evidence that we are defining and treating our women as secondary. If our society assigns women subordinate statuses and roles, does that justly reflect the essential message of the biblical creation found in Genesis 1–3? It is critical to consider and take seriously the real-life experience of our women when we proclaim that we want our Church and society to be biblical.

Furthermore, it is also important to treasure and contemplate the value that tribal communities place on being closely knit, for this is very much a part of our identity. Throughout the history of our traditional patriarchal culture, we have always enjoyed a sense of close community, of living and working together. Everyone looks out for one another, and there are no strangers, there is no homelessness in our kinship system. Village chiefs and now philanthropic organizations line up to care for the widows and orphans. As we saw with the *Lawm*, "corporate weeding," all members of the village—men, women and children—share in both the work and the harvest. As our prominent folktale *Thanghou leh Liandou* teaches us,

---

6. Ibid.

even the orphans who had been taken care of by their aunties and uncles experienced a "new" divine intervention when a snake fell from the sky and turned into a grandmother for the orphan brothers. This grandmother provided and cared for the two boys and they were never in need again. As the story continues, when the time came for the orphan brothers' field to be harvested as part of the *Lawm* co-operative work, the villagers who participated, who had thought that it would only be a morning's work, were surprised by how bountiful the field turned out to be. So, within our traditional patriarchal society, we believe that when members of the community/society are neglected, not treasured, the divine intervenes to help; we believe in a divine benevolence and providence, a divine that values all human beings. Deep within, at the heart and core of our being, we value and believe in the worth of all members of our community. When members of our community are hurting the whole community feels the pain and is affected adversely.

Over and above our own tribal values and beliefs, we believe that our faith, Christianity, and the Bible hold life-affirming messages for all. Those messages, however, may not always be straightforwardly or explicitly spelled out, making it essential to pay close attention to the details in the biblical narratives. Such readings of the Bible should be done with fresh eyes, otherwise we run the risk of misreading what the biblical stories may actually be communicating. It is all too easy to be blinded by what we already assume. This is particularly important since today's Northeast Indian tribal culture shares marked similarities with the ancient Israelite culture. Cautious readings are therefore necessary in our approach to the Bible.

Keitzar also narrates how the tribal worldview has close affinities with that of the ancient Israelites when he alerts us to the critical need for tribal hermeneutics. For instance, Israelite and Northeast Indian tribal cultures are similar in how they relate to nature, natural forces and belief and interaction with supernatural powers.[7] In addition, both the ancient Israelites and tribals today are community-oriented, rooted in kinship relations, with a strong sense of tribal solidarity. Rituals and sacrificial systems of (pre-Christian) tribals are also similar to that of ancient Israelites in many ways. More specifically, the Paite Zomi tribe also has similar systems to the ancient Israelites, notably patriarchy, primogeniture and the *go'el* ("kinsman-redeemer") systems. That tribals share so many similarities with ancient Israelites has, however, both advantages and disadvantages. The similarity is advantageous in that biblical stories do not sound alien

---

7. Keitzar, "Tribal Perspective in Biblical Hermeneutics," 311.

to the lives of tribals and they can fairly easily be related to their lived experiences. The disadvantage of making easy connections between the Bible and tribal culture is that it becomes easy to overlook or fail to appreciate the differences. Caution is needed, as biblical contexts and our contexts today are surely not identical. Therefore, it is crucial to develop approaches and methodologies that are helpful in guiding us in being both faithful to the Scripture as well as being responsible interpreters for our contexts today.

How Then Shall We Read the Bible?

Tribal Christians like the Paites have a Church-oriented and Bible-oriented culture. I share the sincere desire for our cultures and societies to be biblically grounded. I also think such aspirations are to be sought and commended. As a Christian, I strive to be a scriptural person and believe that every genuine Christian individual and community wishes to live biblically. Yet, we are often guilty of applying the qualifier "biblical" to our own standards without the due consideration. Indeed, what qualifies something or someone as "biblical"? Is it when we can quote a few words or verses from the Bible to go alongside our preaching, teaching, customs or the standards we want to promote? Does that make things "biblical"? How can we be more faithful to the Bible? A short answer would be that a faithful reading of the Bible requires us to be cautious about applying biblical texts and messages to our contemporary contexts. Doing so without proper discovery of the original meaning and message of the biblical contexts is certainly to be avoided. In practice, reading and applying Scripture to our lives requires deeper, more reflective study.

I would like to propose three guidelines that I am convinced will be particularly helpful to us tribal Christians in bringing a more faithful and fruitful reading of the Bible. First, I would advocate a shift and broadening of perspective regarding the Bible. Second, I propose re-examining our methods of application. Third, I hope for a balancing out of the central theme(s) and the diverse perspectives contained in the Bible. I will elaborate each point briefly in the following paragraphs.

A Shift and Broadening of Perspective Regarding the Bible

Tribal Christians have very high regard for the Bible, both its completeness and its ready applicability to our daily lives. The physical book of the Bible itself is seen as if it has some magical power to fix all kinds of problems—individual and societal. If we only respect and follow the Bible, all will be fine! On the one hand, the Bible is seen as a spiritual resource, such that revelation from the Holy Spirit is the sole prerequisite for correct biblical interpretation. On the other hand, strong emphasis is placed on its universal relevance, as though straightforward answers to our problems are prestored within it. Such a view of the Bible is not surprising from a practically oriented culture such as the tribal's. And that is indeed how the Bible, the Word of God, comes alive in our lives today, through the Bible impacting our daily lives and struggles. At the same time, such perceptions also often lead us to utilize the Bible as though it is a handy cultural handbook, a code of conduct or a book of doctrine for church and society today. Such simplified views and usages of the Bible result in misinterpretation and misrepresentation of the Scripture. As N. T. Wright rightly cautions, "We cannot reduce scripture to a set of 'timeless truths' on the one hand, or to mere fuel for devotion on the other, without being deeply disloyal, at a structural level, to scripture itself."[8]

The view of the Bible as a straightforward, simplistic and ready-to-apply book needs to be shifted. While it is true that the Bible is applicable for our personal and community lives, understanding what the Bible actually says for us today involves, *in the first instance*, proper contextual study and interpretation. It goes without saying that the ancient Israelites, early Jews and first Christians in their worlds and cultures were quite different from who we are in our modern world today. How can we come to terms with the relevance of the Bible in the biblical times, then throughout the history of Christianity, and then in our lives today? Obviously, taking the terms, statements and stories in the Bible at face value literally will not work, despite our tendency to utilize select terms from the Bible in our attempts to validate our preconceived ideologies. As we saw in the analyses of Genesis 1, 2 and 3, while there are terms that can be misused to argue for subjugation of women—such as "helper," "rule," "because you listened to your wife"—when studied within the wider biblical context these terms and phrases do not imply subjugation. In fact, the theme and message of the whole creation narrative is more life-affirming: that male/man and female/woman are equal, that they share in being made in God's own image and are united in the purpose of being God's representatives. Genesis 1–3 does not promulgate gender subordination, even though we tend to see it that way. It is thus critical to take seriously the negative experiences of our women within Church and wider society, and to genuinely ask ourselves if how we define them and their experience is indeed biblically mandated. When we view

---

8. N. T. Wright, *Scripture and the Authority of God: How to Read the Bible Today* (New York: HarperOne, 2005), 123.

and utilize the Bible irresponsibly to deprive our community members, particularly women, of their authentic God-given worth and value, we become unfaithful to the Scripture.

Let me elaborate further. If we were to accept and practice women's subordination as biblical based on the reasoning that there are a number of stories that (seem to) display women as subordinate, many questions arise. One such question is: Should we implement polygamy as well, since we see it practiced in biblical stories? Despite the fact that polygamy seems to have been common in ancient Israelite culture it is not practiced in our tribal culture today; indeed, we actually condemn cultures practicing polygamy. Patriarchs and prominent leaders of biblical Israel—Abraham, Jacob, Moses, David and others—had more than one wife and are not condemned for it. So would we, then, pronounce polygamy as biblical or as unbiblical? Evidently, it entails a little more discernment and contemplation than simply declaring that something is "biblical" or "unbiblical." This example shows that just as we do not adopt polygamy simply because we see it practiced in the Bible, so also we cannot preach the subordination of women as biblical simply because we observe direct or more subtle traces of it in biblical narratives. We are unfaithful to the Scripture when we perceive and utilize the Bible as a static source of information, a set of examples or rules following which will resolve our specific issues and problems today. As Brueggemann astutely observes, we are perverting the Bible when we regard it "as an answer book or security blanket."[9] Instead, the Bible is a living source that requires engagement, study and conversation.

The Bible as the living Word of God may be likened to a living agent, a person. When building a friendship with someone from a different culture, we understand the person better through conversations and journeying together with them, learning about their background and culture, listening to their perspectives, relating to and comparing with ourselves and so on. In a somewhat similar manner, we may view and approach the Bible as someone that invites our engagement. Through our interaction, engagement and relationship, the Word of God, which we wish to hear through the biblical texts, will speak more authentically. Engaging with biblical texts from that perspective will accordingly shape us and our ways of applying biblical lessons into our contexts today.

It is also necessary to always bear in mind that the divine Word in the Bible is communicated through humans. As Brown suggests, the Bible is

---

9. Walter Brueggemann, *The Bible Makes Sense*, rev. ed. (Louisville: Westminster John Knox Press, 2001), 94.

incarnational, that is, both fully divine and fully human.[10] God communicates to humankind through the Bible, which uses particular language drawn from a particular point of historical time, within particular historical contexts. Parameters such as language, culture, societal norms and systems are not permanent but constantly changing. Therefore, it should not be a surprise to us that the Bible records concepts, references and customs that are clearly distant and different from our linguistic, historical and cultural contexts, despite there sometimes being apparent similarities and synergies. As discussed in the preceding chapters, traditional tribal societies such as the Paite's subscribe to a high view of Scripture and tend to find it easy to fully accept the divine origins of the Bible; the involvement of humans in the Bible's transmission is all too easily skimmed over. Acknowledging that the Bible was produced and reproduced using human means, that it has been translated over and over again using the countless languages of innumerable groups of people, each following the particular cultures and conventions of their particular eras, must surely caution us against simply taking elements from the Bible and applying them literally in modern lives. At the same time, such a recognition will rightly inspire us to examine more fully what the biblical narratives have meant throughout history and what they mean for us now.

In sum, as practically oriented people with a sincere desire to extract practical lessons from the Bible, it is essential for Northeast Indian tribal communities to broaden our perception of the Bible so that we can be ever more faithful to its message. We need to shift away from perceiving and utilizing the Bible as if it is a book of commands or religious laws towards seeing it as a living agent that invites study and engagement. The Bible is the living Word of God communicated through human means at a distinctive historical point of time. As such, it demands our active engagement if we are to follow it with faithfulness and relevance today. It is not to be seen primarily as a static source of doctrinal statements or to hold direct answers to all kinds of problems. Understanding the Bible more fully, viewing the Bible in broader contexts, will positively affect any application of it to our current contexts.

Re-examining our Methods of Application
Following any shift in our perception of the Bible, methods of application also need to be re-examined. This is my second major point. Application, also known as contextualization, can be described as the process of

---

10. Jeannine K. Brown, *Scripture as Communication: Introducing Biblical Hermeneutics* (Grand Rapids: Baker Academic, 2007), 233–4.

making a biblical text or message applicable to our own contexts. Tribal Christians tend to apply Scripture—often with great enthusiasm—to their societies. As practically oriented tribals, merely understanding the stories or statements in the Bible is not enough for us; we want to live them out and make them part of our life and society. This, I think, is the good and right thing to do. Yet also, in our desire to be biblical, it is easy to spot close similarities between our tribal cultures and what the Bible transmits regarding ancient Israelite society. It is all too easy to make hasty connections, assuming that similarity equates to biblical confirmation, sanction or approval. Often, in fact, it is our own culture or situation that is being read back into the Bible, which is then utilized to validate our practices. That being the case, I propose what I will call a "step-back model" in applying Scripture to today's context, particularly tribal Christians: before rushing to apply the Bible in our lives and communities, we must step back and understand the Bible in its own context.

As the present work has hopefully made clear, a Paite coming from a patriarchal culture reading texts like Genesis 2–3 will soon find affinities with his/her own lived experience and context. The reader will relate to the use of "helper" to describe the woman (Gen. 2:18) and understand why "rule" is used for the man (Gen. 3:16). They will look negatively upon the woman for making additions to God's command when she talks to the snake (Gen. 3:3), and will draw negative conclusions from the words "because you listen to your wife" spoken by God to the man (Gen. 3:17). It is easy to associate those terms or phrases in the Bible with the many derogatory labels and sayings our culture and society already have for women, such as "women and fencing are replaceable," "A woman who loiters around is looking for trouble," "Flesh of a crab is no meat; words of a woman are no words," among many others. Reading biblical texts with negative imageries for women already embedded in our society tempts us to easily interpret such texts as if they are instituting the same negative image. Such preconceptions obstruct us from considering carefully the real context and message. As a consequence, perceived affinities with the Bible are used to endorse patriarchal cultural norms such as women's subordinate status as indeed biblical, or even as mandated by the Bible.

Undoubtedly, the negative images of women already embedded in our culture are influential as a lens through which we read and interpret the Bible. What if, instead, we uphold the traces of affirmation that our tribal cultures have/do offer women, using these as a background or focus that informs or stands alongside our reading of the Bible? I believe that it will help us pause and encourage us to read more slowly and closely what the biblical texts and contexts do and do not say before we seek to apply the Bible to our contexts today.

Actually, the hasty association of the Bible with readers' preconceived ideology and cultural expectation is not uncommon. A couple of instances may be mentioned here. Fee and Stuart offer a good example from a Western, English-speaking context. English speakers today easily misunderstand the apostle Paul's use of "flesh" (e.g. Rom. 13:14) as "body" or "bodily appetites." But when the term is studied more closely in its context, Paul can be seen to have been using it as "a spiritual malady, a sickness of spiritual existence."[11] At times, failure to carefully consider the original context can even breed harmful applications of what is taken to be the Bible's teaching. As Sparks reminds us, during the eighteenth and nineteenth centuries slavery was practiced and endorsed in the United States and elsewhere on the basis of the Bible. The southern states took longer to acknowledge slavery as unbiblical, chiefly because of their economic dependence on the slavery system.[12] Critically, the root reason for the practice of slavery was economic need; only secondarily was the Bible commandeered, used as a prop to support the trade in human servitude and misery. When studied in their own contexts, biblical passages that contain references to slaves and slavery (e.g., Exod. 21:20-21; Eph. 6:9; Col. 4:1; Philemon) are not necessarily promoting the practice of slavery; rather, they are reflecting what was practiced in the society of that time. The mere fact that some biblical texts mention slaves, and even advise how to be a God-fearing slave or slave owner, does not mean that the Bible advocates, condones or grants permission for it in our contexts today.

Biblical narratives deal first and foremost with issues pertaining to their times, not ours, and their solutions do not necessarily answer the specific questions that arise in our lives today.[13] That does not mean their "solutions" cannot be relevant to us today. What it means is that we cannot transfer them directly to our situations without first understanding the original contexts and our context. To reiterate the need to step back into the narrative's context in its own terms, we may briefly consider Genesis 1–3 within the larger ancient Near Eastern context. (We have analyzed Gen. 1–3 within its literary context in the preceding chapters.) When read within the larger historical and cultural setting of the ancient Near East, establishing the subordinate status of female/women does not seem to be the goal of Genesis 1–3. Instead, what is central to the creation of Genesis

11. Gordon D. Fee and Douglas Stuart, *How to Read the Bible for All Its Worth: A Guide to Understanding the Bible* (Grand Rapids: Zondervan, 1982), 16–17.
12. Kenton L. Sparks, *God's Word in Human Words: An Evangelical Appropriation of Critical Biblical Scholarship* (Grand Rapids: Baker Academic, 2008), 289–90.
13. Fee and Stuart, *How to Read the Bible*, 76–8.

1–3 is how the biblical God created all human beings equally in the same image and likeness of God. With that theme, Genesis 1–3 is distinct from other ancient Near Eastern creation stories, which typically regard kings as the sole image-bearers of the divine. Also, while other ancient Near Eastern creation stories record that human beings were formed with the express purpose of serving as the slaves of the gods who created them, in Genesis 1–3 human beings are created with intimate care and attention by God—a notable difference that reflects a cordial relationship with God. Thus, exploring the larger context helps us to see that any preaching within cultures that see one group of humanity (females) as lower in status than another group of humanity (males) is decidedly unbiblical. What we actually see is that such preaching and practice aligns with the non-biblical ancient Near East stories and their hierarchical concepts—which the biblical creation story differentiated itself from.

The above observations cohere with our findings from the literary analysis of Genesis 1–3. Therefore, understanding humanity within the literary context of the biblical creation narrative, as well as its broader historical context, challenges us to take seriously our tribal women's negative experiences. It also compels us to reconsider whether instituting the modern-day subordination of women as biblically established at creation is truly a faithful reading of the text.

Approaching the biblical text with a requirement that it receives prior and appropriate analysis before its application to our lived contexts applies equally to all genres found in the Bible. Be it narrative, prophecy, poetry, apocalyptic or any other genre, it is crucial to approach each text as requiring advance understanding of its own particular historical context. Each biblical narrative is set within its own setting, one that will be different from the one(s) we inhabit, be that in terms of language, culture or societal assumption. Each biblical prophecy was proclaimed using forms of language and methods of illustration that were particular to its historical setting, ones that may not be transferable easily to our modern times. Similarly, poetry and apocalyptic literature in the Bible were written from within particular historical contexts using metaphorical and/or allegorical languages that may seem strange to us today. As such, it is important to understand that the Bible, in any genre, was first produced within particular settings, intended for (a) specific target audience(s). The biblical stories often point to a world very different from our own in many ways, though at times they appear to offer points of connection…on the superficial level. Tribal Christians in particular need to step back before applying the biblical text to their lives. That tribal Christians seemingly share so many things with the ancient Israelite culture, as this is presented in the Bible, should not be taken at face value.

Equally important is the sensitive study of our own lived contexts. Understanding our own settings better will surely help us to discern how biblical lessons may be applied valuably and responsibly to our own lives. Many others have made this important point. In comprehending our own contexts, we should also appreciate the nuances of our own cultural, historical and other landscapes; we should not rush to simply criticize or disrespect.[14] For instance, the deep sense of community, as opposed to individualism, that we in tribal societies possess is traditional and is to be treasured, preserved and upheld—it is integral to our sense of community, which values and seeks the well-being of all its members. Then, treasuring and preserving the life-affirming values we already have in our culture and putting those values in conversation with biblical stories, we need to envision ways to build a faithful biblical society. As Brueggemann puts it succinctly, as readers of the Bible we have to be both "historical and imaginative."[15] That is, in addition to stepping back and studying the biblical stories on their own terms, it is necessary to consider ways to implement what the biblical stories teach us meaningfully in our lives today. A preliminary question that may be asked is, Do our cultures and societies, with the subordination of women, truly reflect the biblical and Christian message?

I must clarify that in practice the two steps of exploring the original contexts of the biblical texts and applying biblical lessons to our daily lives may not happen as discrete, scientific steps. It may not be possible to first resolve all the contextual questions of the biblical texts, close that step and then move on to studying our current contexts today. As Brown contends, the steps of exegesis (studying the biblical texts) and contextualization (applying to our own contexts) are fluid and complex.[16] The two steps do not necessarily progress in a singular, linear fashion, as though moving from point A to point B in succession. They are more of a process and journey, more like moving back and forth; the route(s) taken may be circular or intertwined. Words I might employ for the "first" step, studying the biblical texts, such as "prior to" or "before," do not strictly imply precedence in time. Often, we approach the Bible faced with issues and challenges, and we search the text for discernment and biblical answers and resolution. In those circumstances, it is tempting to find easy solutions

14. Wright, *Scripture and the Authority of God*, 129.
15. Brueggemann, *The Bible Makes Sense*, 15.
16. Brown, *Scripture as Communication*, 234–8.

based on apparently similar situations appearing in the Bible. However, it is necessary to dwell in and understand the biblical story in its own context before prematurely extracting or transferring "lessons" to our specific issues today.

I cannot stress too much the need for a deep understanding of the biblical texts and contexts, as well as a full appreciation for how our own contexts may actually differ from the setting(s) of the biblical text. Full consideration of these matters must be given before making strong claims about whether something is biblical, and before rigidly applying any such biblical teaching to our own context today. When we step back and examine the biblical texts carefully in their own contexts and study our own contexts carefully, we can see that our current beliefs and practices may not necessarily be biblically mandated. Biblical narratives do not promulgate gender subjugation or slavery. Where these practices show up in the Bible, it is a reflection of the societal settings of the biblical texts. This being the case, I agree with N. T. Wright's suggestion that we should study the way things were, as described in the biblical narratives, and implement it today according to "the way things should be."[17] Admittedly, "the way things should be" is not always easy to determine and agree upon—and harder still to put into practice. Yet that is actually further confirmation that the Bible and its contexts need to be studied diligently before transferring any biblical message to our own contemporary contexts. Being truly faithful to the Bible involves being open to the fact that biblical narratives derived from times and contexts that were (sometimes significantly) different from our own. Importantly, applying the message of the Bible, living a biblical life, can only be achieved through careful consideration of the overall message of the Bible, rather than on the basis of short, decontextualized sections of biblical text.

Central Theme and Variety of Perspectives Within the Bible
Another crucial requirement, which goes alongside the need to step back before applying the Bible in our daily lives, is the acceptance that the biblical narratives themselves can offer differing perspectives on a given issue. The Bible contains both a central theme and a diversity of viewpoints. As readers, it is easy to prioritize one theme or particular view within the Bible, aligning it with our ideology and using it to trump other passages which express differing or opposing views. For instance, in the case of gender issues, it is easy for a reader with a preconceived hierarchical ideology to prioritize passages that appear to present women as subordinate over those which elevate women. And *vice versa*.

---

17. Wright, *Scripture and the Authority of God*, 124.

Arguments are often made that women's subordination and men's higher status and headship is biblical by drawing inferences from stories where women appear to be in subordinate positions, as well as other details. For example, the omission of the names of wives and daughters from Old Testament genealogies has been used to support the view that women had a lesser status, that they were unimportant. This, certainly, is a reflection of ancient Israel's patriarchal and patrilineal culture. On the other hand, alternative conclusions can be drawn upon a careful reading of the Bible as a whole. Quite simply, nowhere in the Old Testament is there evidence of a woman being denied high status or a leadership role over men simply because she is a female/woman. Needless to say, stories in the Old Testament reflect a principally patriarchal culture with predominantly male leadership; but that does not mean that such is the approved biblical way. Rather, it is a reflection of the culture and society of a particular people group—the ancient Israelites. In fact, if we read carefully and consider deeply the experience of the women in biblical stories under their patriarchal norms, we can see that many of the biblical accounts reveal how the patriarchal norms failed women and wider society, sometimes tragically.

It is also beyond denial that God used both women and men to lead God's people. For instance, Miriam was called a "prophetess" and was charged by God to lead Israel (Exod. 15:20; Mic. 6:4). Deborah was one of the judges God used to deliver victory for the Israelites. She commanded Israel's male army commander Barak (Judg 4–5), and was a prophetess while also being a wife and a mother (Judg. 4:4; 5:7). The prophetess Huldah was consulted and obeyed by priests and kings in their search for the lost book of the law, the discovery of which brought about a cultic reform (2 Kgs 22:14–23:3). In an Old Testament book bearing her name, Queen Esther was the savior of the Jews.

So far we have looked only at the Old Testament. At this point it will be helpful to briefly examine further references from the New Testament.

Passages such as 1 Cor. 14:34-35 or 1 Tim. 2:11-15 appear to prescribe the silencing of women and seem to exclude women from positions of authority and teaching within Christian communities.[18] Yet also, alternate

---

18. 1 Cor. 14:34-35 expresses that women should remain silent in churches, saving any questions they might have for home, since, "as the law says," it is a disgrace for a woman to speak at church. And, 1 Tim. 2:11-14 expresses that a woman should learn in quietness and submission: "I do not permit a woman to teach or have authority over a man since Adam was formed first, then Eve, the woman was deceived to become a sinner; women will be saved through childbearing if they remain in faith, love and holiness."

views are observable within the same chapter and book. Several verses in 1 Corinthians 14 (such as vv. 5, 24, 26, 31, 39) affirm that "all, everyone" are able to teach and prophesy. And if 1 Tim. 2:11-15 is taken literally as a directive for women to remain silent, in the next chapter, 1 Tim. 3:2, 12, we encounter the suggestion that overseers and deacons are to be married men with one wife. This opens up several questions: Does this mean that single men cannot lead the church? And what happens if the wife of a deacon or overseer dies? Is he to stand down?

Elsewhere, there are passages that proclaim mutuality and sameness of males/men and females/women. 1 Corinthians 11:11-12 declares that in the Lord neither woman nor man are independent of each other; just as a woman came from man, man also is born of woman. Galatians 3:28 states there is no male nor female—all are one in Christ.

To take one more example, passages such as Eph. 5:22 and Col. 3:18 are frequently quoted to preach wives' submission to husbands. Strikingly, however, generally only the submission of the wife is emphasized. As such, a picture is created whereby wives/women, simply on the basis of their being wives/women, ought to submit to their husbands, simply on the basis of their husbands/men. Forbearance and submission of the woman/wife is offered as if it supplies the antidote to any abusive actions of an abusive husband! The next verses give a fuller picture: husbands ought to love their wives, just as Christ loves the Church (Eph. 5:25; Col. 3:19) and sacrifices for her (Eph. 5:25). Therefore, when considered as a whole, mutuality between the sexes can be seen.

Finally, just as female prophets are found and named in the Old Testament, so too we have female prophets and apostles mentioned in the New: Anna (Lk. 2:36), Philip's daughters (Acts 21:9) and Junia (Rom. 16:7). These *women*, notably, are not condemned for their *active religious participation*—indeed, they are actually praised.

The above examples plainly show that there is no single, unified or established biblical rule that women are inherently the subordinate gender and men are the authoritative head. While one reader might cite a selection of biblical verses to claim women's subordination is biblical, another is able to cite different verses to claim otherwise. A critical question, then, is whether lifting one statement up, taking it as absolute and having a veto over others, is being faithful to the Bible. This question brings us back to our point for the need to study each biblical statement or passage in its own contexts. As we have seen, once texts are studied by situating them within their own contexts, any apparent power to subjugate falls away, and the superficiality of narrow reading becomes evident. As I have argued, it is vital to consider diligently the overall theme and message of the whole

Bible, which, I contend, contains an obvious and undeniable overarching theme that all members of humanity have equal worth and value, as each is created in God's own image, as a member of Christ's body, the Church. At the very least, the subordination of women is not the central theme of the whole Bible when it comes to issues of gender relation.

It is important to be self-conscious of our preconceived ideologies and make every effort to read the narratives with open, clear minds. In other words, we should be ready to be offended by the Bible and not afraid to wrestle with it, testing our own preconceived standpoints as well as the different viewpoints within the Bible itself. As a general guideline, in cases of differing or polar views within the Bible, we should consider the overall message of the whole Scripture, a method which Sparks terms a "sensible canonical approach" or what Brueggemann calls "central direction."[19] Wright neatly writes that "A properly contextual reading of scripture will celebrate the rich diversity of material within the canon, resisting attempts to flatten it out into a monochrome uniformity, while at the same time always looking for the larger unity within which different emphases are held together."[20] That is, as much as we tend to uphold the terms and passages that seem to support women's subjugation, we also ought to consider the passages that assert the equal status of men and women. And with that, consideration of any differing or seemingly opposing teachings within the overarching theme of the Bible needs to be against the backdrop of an (ideally prior) investigation of the immediate contexts of each passage or pericope. This seems to me to be a safe path towards the faithful reading and responsible application of the Scripture.

It is also important to note that alternative perspectives exist not just within the Bible itself. Multiple readings of a given biblical text are, quite naturally, produced by different cultures today. One passage that means something to one culture or community may mean something different to another community. For instance, a critical question that arises is: While members of a patriarchal Christian community might read Genesis 2–3 as supporting gender-based systems of hierarchy, how would a matriarchal community read the same text? And how would members of patriarchal communities receive the readings of matriarchal or egalitarian Christian communities? Would patriarchal Christians render the divergent readings as un-biblical or un-Christian? Another related and difficult question is: How can we be truly biblical while also being true to our rich heritage

---

19. Sparks, *God's Word in Human Words*, 353; Brueggemann, *The Bible Makes Sense*, 97.

20. Wright, *Scripture and the Authority of God*, 129.

and culture? And indeed, are we actually able to achieve this? Truthful engagement with such vital questions should journey alongside careful study of biblical narratives as well as serious reflection about our contemporary cultures. Then, testing and contemplating those questions with the central and overall message of the whole Bible should lead us closer to understanding what is truly biblical.

A question to consider as a starting point might be this: Does, or could, a patriarchal culture (or a matriarchal or egalitarian one, for that matter) genuinely affirm and ensure that the true worth, essence and status of all its members plays out it in each one's lived experience? Because, if we preach that the Bible teaches that God creates every human being, male and female, equally in God's own image, and that Jesus died for all and loves every last person, but then accept, institute and maintain practices that denigrate and subjugate members of our community, we clearly have a contradiction. Such practices will be at odds with what is understood to be biblical, and what it is to be a biblical Christian.

In interpreting the Bible, then, not only should we be in conversation with the Bible, but we should also be in conversation with other interpretations. We should approach the Scripture with the utmost humility and with an acceptance of our limitedness as individual humans, as members of one finite culture among many others. We can only gain wisdom and get (closer) to the width and depth of the true meaning(s) of Scripture with such a humble, sincere and open-minded approach to the Bible. That will help us in applying the Bible more faithfully in our contexts, and allow us to engage with Scripture in more responsible ways that will be life affirming for all.

Bibliography

Alter, Robert. *Genesis: Translation and Commentary.* New York: W. W. Norton, 1996.
Alter, Robert. *The Hebrew Bible: A Translation with Commentary, Vol. 1: The Five Books of Moses.* New York: W. W. Norton, 2019.
Angami, Zhodi. *Tribals, Empire and God: A Tribal Reading of the Birth of Jesus in Matthew's Gospel.* London: Bloomsbury T&T Clark, 2017.
Ao, Temsula. "'Benevolent Subordination': Social Status of Naga Women." In *The Peripheral Centre: Voices From India's Northeast*, edited by Preeti Gill, 100–107. New Delhi: Zubaan, 2010.
Arnold, Bill T. *Genesis.* NCBC. New York: Cambridge University Press, 2009.
Barr, Beth Allison. *The Making of Biblical Womanhood: How the Subjugation of Women Became the Gospel Truth.* Grand Rapids: Brazos Press, 2021.
Basumatary, Songram. *Ethnicity and Tribal Theology: Problems and Prospects for Peaceful Co-existence in Northeast India.* Oxford: Peter Lang, 2015.
Bennett, Judith M. *History Matters: Patriarchy and the Challenge of Feminism.* Philadelphia: University of Pennsylvania Press, 2006.
Bird, Phyllis A. "'Male and Female He Created Them': Gen 1:27b in the Context of the Priestly Account of Creation." *HTR* 74.2 (1981): 129–59.
Brown, Jeannine K. *Scripture as Communication: Introducing Biblical Hermeneutics.* Grand Rapids: Baker Academic, 2007.
Brueggemann, Walter. *The Bible Makes Sense.* Rev. ed. Louisville: Westminster John Knox Press, 2001.
Cassuto, U. *A Commentary on the Book of Genesis, Volume 1.* Translated by Israel Abrahams. Jerusalem: Magnes, 1972.
Clines, David J. A. "אדם, The Hebrew for 'Human, Humanity': A Response to James Barr." *VT* 53, no. 3 (2003): 297–310.
Clines, David J. A. *On the Way to the Postmodern: Old Testament Essays 1967–1998, Volume 2.* London: Bloomsbury Publishing, 1998.
Clines, David J. A. *What Does Eve Do to Help? And Other Readerly Questions to the Old Testament.* JSOTSup 94. Sheffield: JSOT Press, 1990.
Clines, David J. A., ed. *The Dictionary of Classical Hebrew.* Sheffield: Sheffield Academic Press, 2001.
Condren, Janson C. "Toward a Purge of the Battle of the Sexes and 'Return' for the Original Meaning of Genesis 3:16b." *JETS* 60, no. 2 (2017): 227–45.
Cooper, T. T. *New Routes for Commerce: The Mishmee Hills (1873).* London: Henry S. King & Co., 1873.
Dearman, J. Andrew. *Reading Hebrew Bible Narratives.* Oxford: Oxford University Press, 2019.

Dena, Lal. *Christian Missions and Colonialism: A Study of Missionary Movement in Northeast India With Particular Reference to Manipur and Lushai Hills 1894–1947.* Shillong: Vendrame Institute, 1988.

Downs, Frederick. S. "Christian Conversion Movements in North East India." In *Religious Conversion in India: Modes, Motivations, and Meanings*, edited by Rowena Robinson and Sathianathan Clarke, 381–400. Oxford: Oxford University Press, 2003.

Downs, Frederick. S. "Christianity and Socio-Cultural Change in the Hill Areas of North East India." *ICHR* 26, no. 1 (1992): 50–62.

Downs, Frederick. S. *The Christian Impact on the Status of Women in North East India: Professor H. K. Barpujari Endowment Lectures.* Shillong: North-Eastern Hill University Publications, 1996.

Downs, Frederick. S. "Christianity as a Tribal Response to Change in Northeast India." *Missiology: An International Review* 8, no. 4 (1980): 408–16.

Downs, Frederick. S. "Early Christian Contacts with North East India." *ICHR* 5, no. 1 (1971): 44–69.

Downs, Frederick. S. "Faith and Life-style: How Christianity was Understood by Nineteenth Century Converts in North East India." *Bangalore Theological Forum* 14, no.1 (Jan.–June 1982): 20–43.

Downs, Frederick. S. *History of Christianity in India, Volume 5, Part 5: Northeast India in the Nineteenth and Twentieth Centuries.* Bangalore: The Church History Association of India, 1992.

Elwin, Verrier, ed. *India's North-East Frontier in the Nineteenth Century.* Bombay: Oxford University Press, 1959.

Fee, Gordon D., and Douglas Stuart. *How To Read the Bible for All Its Worth: A Guide to Understanding the Bible.* Grand Rapids: Zondervan, 1982.

Fiorenza, Elisabeth Schüssler. "Biblical Interpretation and Kyriarchal Globalization." In *The Oxford Handbook of Feminist Approaches to the Hebrew Bible*, edited by Susan Scholz, 3–20. Oxford: Oxford University Press, 2020.

Foh, Susan T. "What is the Woman's Desire." *WTJ* 37 (1975): 376–83.

Fretheim, Terence E. *Genesis.* New Interpreter's Bible 1. Nashville: Abingdon Press, 2004.

Grierson, George Abraham. *Languages of North-Eastern India, Volume 2.* New Delhi: Gyan Publishing House, 1995.

Grudem, Wayne. *Evangelical Feminism and Biblical Truth: An Analysis of More Than One Hundred Disputed Questions.* Wheaton: Crossway, 2012.

Guite, Mercy Vungthianmuang, and Grace Donnemching. "Gender Representation in Folklore Culture: Dissection of Selected Paite Tribe of Manipur." *Political Economy Journal of India* 26.1 (Jan-June 2017): 80–6.

Hanghal, Ninglun. "A Gender Perspective on Democratisation." In *Democratisation Process in North-East India: Some Issues and Challenges*, edited by S. Thianlalmuan Ngaihte and L. T. Sasang Guite, 73–83. New Delhi: Gyan Publishing House, 2015.

Hangzo, Tara Manchin. "Gender Equality among the Zomis." In *Democratisation Process in North-East India: Some Issues and Challenges*, edited by S. Thianlalmuan Ngaihte and L. T. Sasang Guite, 51–71. New Delhi: Gyan Publishing House, 2015.

Hess, Richard S. "Equality With and Without Innocence." In *Discovering Biblical Equality: Complementarity Without Hierarchy*, edited by Ronald W. Pierce and Rebecca Merrill Groothuis, 79–95. 2nd ed. Downers Grove: IVP Academic, 2005.

Hiebert, Theodore. "'God Saw How Beautiful It Was': Creation in the Bible as Science, Art, and Theology." In *The Earth is the Lord's: Essays on Creation and the Bible in Honor of Ben C. Ollenburger*, edited by Ryan D. Harker and Heather L. Bunce, 3–16. Philadelphia: Eisenbrauns, 2019.

Hminthanzuali, "Bride Price and Patriarchal Hegemony in the Mizo Society." In *Gender Lens: Women's Issues and Perspectives*, edited by Rekha Pande, 377–92. New Delhi: Rawat Publications, 2015.

Holladay, William Lee. *A Concise Hebrew and Aramaic Lexicon of the Old Testament: Based upon the Lexical Work of Ludwig Koehler and Walter Baumgartner.* Grand Rapids: Eerdmans, 1971.

Jamir, Shiluinla. "State, Patriarchy and Gender: Everyday Resistance of Women in the Borderland (Northeast India)." *Religion and Society* 63, no. 1 (2018): 66–81.

Johnson, Allan G. *The Gender Knot: Unraveling Our Patriarchal Legacy.* 3rd ed. Philadelphia: Temple University Press, 2014.

Kamkhenthang, H. "Christianity *vis-à-vis* Tribal Religion in Manipur." In *Religion in Northeast India*, edited by Soumen Sen, 39–46. New Delhi: Uppal Publishing House, 1993.

Kamkhenthang, H. *The Paite: A Transborder Tribe of India and Burma.* New Delhi: Mittal Publications, 1988.

Kamkhenthang, H. "Role of Women in the Customary Practices of the Paite." In *Gender Implications of Tribal Customary Law: The Case of North-East India*, edited by Melvil Pereira et al., 162–70. New Delhi: Rawat Publications, 2017.

Keitzar, Renthy. "A Study of the North-East Indian Tribal Christian Theology." In *Society and Culture in North-East India: A Christian Perspective*, edited by Saral K. Chatterji, 118–27. Delhi: Indian Society for Promoting Christian Knowledge, 1996.

Keitzar, Renthy. "Tribal Perspective in Biblical Hermeneutics Today." *IJT* 31, no. 3–4 (1982): 293–313.

Key, Andrew F. "The Giving of Proper Names in the Old Testament." *JBL* 83 no. 1 (1964): 55–9.

Khanna, S. K. *Encyclopaedia of North-East India: Arunachal Pradesh, Assam, Manipur, Meghalaya, Tripura, Sikkim, Mizoram, Nagaland.* Delhi: Indian Publishers' Distributors, 1999.

Khupkhothang, *Chanchinpha Vak Hun Pawlut Masate* [Those Who First Brought the Good News Light]. Churachandpur: Evangelical Organization Church, 1992.

Kraus, Helen. *Gender Issues in Ancient and Reformation Translations of Genesis 1–4.* Oxford: Oxford University Press, 2011.

Lalmuoklien. *Gospel Through Darkness: The History and the Missionary Work of the Northeast India General Mission (now ECCI) 1910–2004.* Churachandpur: Self-published, 2009.

Lamdbin, Thomas O. *Introduction to Biblical Hebrew.* 1973. 19th Printing, London: Darton, Longman & Todd, 2009.

Lee-Barnewall, Michelle. *Neither Complementarian nor Egalitarian: A Kingdom Corrective to the Evangelical Gender Debate.* Grand Rapids: Baker Academic, 2016.

Liankhohau, T. *Social, Cultural, Economic and Religious Life of a Transformed Community: A Study of Paite Tribe.* New Delhi: Mittal Publications, 1994.

Lohr, Joel N. "Sexual Desire? Eve, Genesis 3:16 and תשׁוקה." *JBL* 130, no. 2 (2011): 227–46.

Lorrain, J. Herbert, and F. W. Savidge. "After Ten Years: Report for 1913 of the BMS Mission in South Lushai Hills, Assam." In *The Annual Report of BMS on Mizoram 1901–1938.* Serkawrn: Mizoram Gospel Centenary Committee, 1994.

Luai Chin Thang. "A History of the Evangelical Baptist Convention Among the Paite Tribe in North East India." Unpublished D.min. Dissertation: Reformed Theological Seminary, Jackson, MI, 2000.

Macintosh, A. A. "The Meaning of the Hebrew תשוקה." *JSS* 61, no. 2 (2016): 365–87.

Matskevich, Karalina. *Construction of Gender and Identity in Genesis: The Subject and the Other.* New York: T&T Clark, 2019.

Meyers, Carol L. "Gender and the Heterarchy Alternative for Re-Modeling Ancient Israel." In *The Oxford Handbook of Feminist Approaches to the Hebrew Bible*, edited by Susanne Scholz, 443–59. Oxford: Oxford University Press, 2020.

Meyers, Carol L. "Gender Roles and Genesis 3:16 Revisited." In *A Feminist Companion to Genesis*, edited by Athalya Brenner, 118–41. Sheffield: Sheffield Academic Press, 1993.

Meyers, Carol L. "Hierarchy or Heterarchy? Archaeology and the Theorizing of Israelite Society." In *Confronting the Past: Archaeological and Historical Essays in Honor of William G. Dever*, edited by Seymour Gitin, J. P. Dessel, and J. Edward Wright, 245–54. Winona Lake: Eisenbrauns, 2006.

Meyers, Carol L. *Rediscovering Eve: Ancient Israelite Women in Context.* Oxford: Oxford University Press, 2013.

Miller, Pavla. *Patriarchy.* New York: Routledge, 2017.

Morris, John Hughes. *The History of the Welsh Calvinistic Methodists' Foreign Mission, to the End of the Year 1904.* Carnarvon: C. M. Book Room, 1910.

Nembiakkim, Rose. *Reproductive Health Awareness among the Tribal Women in Manipur.* New Delhi: Concept Publishing, 2008.

Ngaihte, S. Thianlalmuan, and Kaba Daniel. "Discourse on Tradition and Modernity among the Paite." In *NEIHA: Proceedings, 32nd Session, 2011.* https://papers.ssrn.com/sol3/papers.cfm?abstract_id=2173701.

Ngaihte, S. Thianlalmuan. *Elite, Identity and Politics in Manipur.* New Delhi: Mittal Publications, 2013.

Ortlund, Raymond C. Jr. "Male–Female Equality and Male Headship: Genesis 1–3." In *Recovering Biblical Manhood and Womanhood: A Response to Evangelical Feminism*, edited by John Piper and Wayne Grudem, 119–41. Wheaton: Crossway, 2021.

Otwell, John H. *And Sarah Laughed: The Status of Woman in the Old Testament.* Philadelphia: Westminster Press, 1977.

Paite Tribe Council General Headquarters. *The Paite Customary Law & Practices 2nd Amendment, 2013.* Lamka, Manipur: Paite Tribe Council, 2013.

Phaipi, Ashley Nengsuanthang. "Mission Transformation for Evangelical Baptist Convention, India: From Evangelistic Approach to Integral Mission." Unpublished DMin Dissertation, Lutheran School of Theology at Chicago, 2018.

Ralte, Lalrinawmi. "Patriarchy and Christianity in the Mizo Church: A Feminist Critique." *Bangalore Theological Forum* 31, no. 1 (1999): 117–33.

Ramsey, George W. "Is Name-Giving an Act of Domination in Gen 2:23 and Elsewhere?" *CBQ* 50 (1988): 24–35.

Ray, Asok Kumar. "Tribal Women in North-East India." In *Gender Implications of Tribal Customary Law: The Case of North-East India*, edited by Melvil Pereira, R. P. Athparia et al., 46–53. New Delhi: Rawat Publications, 2017.

Rodrigues, Shaunna. "Negotiating Equality: Endorsing Women's Rights through Customary Laws." In *Gender Implications of Tribal Customary Law: The Case of North-East India*, edited by Melvil Pereira, R. P. Athparia et al., 71–83. New Delhi: Rawat Publications, 2017.
Sarna, Nahum. *Genesis.* JPS Torah Commentary. Philadelphia: Jewish Publication Society, 1989.
Schmitt, John J. "Like Eve, Like Adam: *mšl* in Gen 3,16." *Bib* 72, no. 1 (1991): 1–22.
Shakespear, J. *The Lushei Kuki Clans.* Aizawl, Mizoram: Tribal Research Institute, 1975.
Shinkhokam, *Pu-Pa Nun* [Life of Forefathers]. Lamka: Self Published, 2005.
Siamkhum, Th. *The Paites: A Study of the Changing Faces of the Community.* Chennai: Notion Press, 2013.
Singh, Karam Manmohan. *History of the Christian Missions in Manipur and Neighbouring States.* New Delhi: Mittal Publications, 1991.
Singh, K. S. *The Scheduled Tribes.* People of India National Series 3. Delhi: Oxford University Press, 1994.
Sparks, Kenton L. *God's Word in Human Words: An Evangelical Appropriation of Critical Biblical Scholarship.* Grand Rapids: Baker Academic, 2008.
Speiser, E. A. *Genesis.* AB 1. New York: Doubleday, 1964.
Thangtungnung, H., and S. Ngulzadal, *History of Paite Literature.* https://www.academia.edu/34934290/HISTORY_OF_PAITE_LITERATURE. Accessed on February 10, 2022.
Thanzauva, and R. L. Hnuni. "Ethnicity, Identity and Hermeneutics: An Indian Tribal Perspective." In *Ethnicity and the Bible*, edited by Mark G. Brett, 343–57. Boston: Brill Academic Publishers, 2002.
Trible, Phyllis. *God and the Rhetoric of Sexuality.* Philadelphia: Fortress Press, 1978.
Vogels, Walter. "The Power Struggle between Man and Woman (Gen 3:16b)." *Bib* 77 (1996): 197–209.
Von Rad, Gerhard. *Genesis: A Commentary.* Rev. ed. OTL. Philadelphia: Westminster Press, 1976.
Webb, William J. *Slaves, Women & Homosexuals: Exploring the Hermeneutics of Cultural Analysis.* Downers Grove: InterVarsity Press, 2001.
Wenham, Gordon. *Genesis.* WBC. Dallas: Word Books, 1987.
Wright, N. T. *Scripture and the Authority of God: How to Read the Bible Today.* New York: HarperOne, 2005.
Zevit, Ziony. *What Really Happened in the Garden of Eden?* New Haven: Yale University Press, 2013.
Zhimomi, Kaholi. "Northeast India." In *Christianity in South and Central Asia*, edited by Kenneth R. Ross, Daniel Jeyaraj, and Todd M. Johnson, 156–67. Edinburgh: Edinburgh University Press, 2019.

Index of References

**Hebrew Bible/
Old Testament**
Genesis
1–3	4, 61, 97, 109, 114, 117, 121, 122	1:26-28	63, 64, 68, 70, 75–7, 109	2:22	80, 87
		1:26-27	65, 67	2:23-24	86
		1:26	62, 63, 65–7, 70, 71, 75, 77	2:23	86, 87, 89–91
				2:24	90, 99
1	4, 63–6, 69, 74, 76–9, 92, 94, 107, 109, 110, 117	1:27	65–7, 70, 74	3	4, 62, 63, 77, 78, 92–5, 104–7, 110, 117
		1:28	66, 67, 70, 71, 75–7		
		1:31	64	3:1-12	94
		2–3	101, 109, 120, 127	3:1	94
1:1–2:4	64			3:2-3	94
1:1-25	70	2	4, 62, 63, 77–81, 85, 91–4, 100, 107, 109, 110, 117	3:3	93, 120
1:1-2	65			3:6	93–5, 99, 105
1:3-25	71				
1:3	65			3:12	95, 99
1:5	66			3:13	105
1:6	65, 66	2:4-25	64, 80	3:14-19	102
1:7	65	2:4	64	3:14	96
1:9	65	2:5	106	3:15	102, 105
1:11	65, 66	2:7	56, 80, 84	3:16	62, 63, 93, 96–104, 106, 110, 120
1:12	66	2:9	106		
1:14-16	66	2:15	102, 106		
1:14	65	2:16-17	94, 105	3:17-19	93, 104, 105
1:15	65	2:18	79, 80, 82–4, 95, 104, 120		
1:16-18	103			3:17	96, 97, 102, 105, 106, 120
1:16	69				
1:20-23	65	2:19-23	84		
1:20	65, 66	2:19-20	84, 87, 99	3:19	102, 105
1:21	65, 66	2:19	84	3:20	88
1:22	66	2:20	80, 88, 90, 104	4:1-16	85
1:24	65, 66			4:1	104
1:25	66	2:21-22	84, 86	4:7	97–9
		2:21	80	4:25	104

5:1-2	76	48:12-20	85	*Judges*	
5:28-29	88	48:22-26	85	4–5	125
5:29	97			4:4	125
6:9	80	*Exodus*		5:7	125
9:1	76	3:12	95	8:22-23	103
10:1	80	4:8-9	105	14:4	103
11:10	80	10:10	83	15:11	103
13:1	95	15:20	125	18:29	88
16:2	104	18:4	82		
16:5	104	21:20-21	121	*Ruth*	
16:6	104	22:8	103	1:14	90
16:11	88	23:5	90		
16:13	88	25:12	86	*1 Samuel*	
16:15	85	26:26	86	6:5	72
17:19-22	85	26:27	86	6:11	72
18:16	95	36:25	86		
21:10-12	104	36:31	86	*2 Samuel*	
21:22	95	36:32	86	5:1	87
25:12	80	37:3	86	8:5	83
25:23	85	37:5	86	16:13	86
25:25	88	38:7	86	19:13	87
25:27	85			20:2	90
29:14	86	*Leviticus*		23:3	101
29:32	88	25:43	73	23:10	90
29:33	88	25:46	73		
29:34	88	25:53	73	*1 Kings*	
29:35	88	26:17	73	4:21 Eng.	103
30:6	88			5:1	103
30:8	88	*Numbers*		6:5	86
30:11	88	24:19	73	6:6	86
30:13	88	33:52	72	6:15	86
30:18	88			6:16	86
30:20	88	*Deuteronomy*		6:34	86
31:30	98	3:14	88	11:2	90
31:32	83	15:6	103	16:24	88
31:37	83	33:7	82	20:16	83
34:3	90	33:26	82	21:13	83
37:27	87	33:29	82	22:19	71
38:29	88				
38:30	88	*Joshua*		*2 Kings*	
41:45	89	3:16	83	11:18	72
41:51	88	7:24	95	16:10	72
41:52	88	10:33	83	22:14–23:3	125
45:8	103	12:2	103	23:34	89
45:26	103	12:5	103	24:17	89
47:15	83	19:47	88		

Index of References

1 Chronicles	
5:1-2	85
12:21 Eng.	83
12:22	83
29:12	103

2 Chronicles	
9:26	103
20:6	103

Nehemiah	
3:8	90
3:34	90

Esther	
1:22	103

Job	
30:19	101
38:7	71
41:25	101
41:33 Eng.	102

Psalms	
20:2 Eng.	82
20:3	82
22:28 Eng.	103
22:29	103
28:1	101
33:20	82
38:17 Eng.	83
38:18	83
44:15 Eng.	83
44:16	83
49:13	101
49:21	101
51:3 Eng.	83
51:5	83
59:13 Eng.	103
59:14	103
70:5 Eng.	82
70:6	82
72:8	73
103:19	103
107:9	98
110:2	73
115:9	82
115:10	82
115:11	82
121:1	82
121:2	82
124:8	82
127:2	96
136:8-9	103
146:5 Eng.	82
146:6	82

Proverbs	
5:10	96
14:23	96
15:1	96
16:32	103

Song of Songs	
7:10	99
7:11	97, 98
7:11 Eng.	99

Isaiah	
13:8	96
14:2	73
21:3	96
26:17	96
26:18	96
29:8	98
30:5	82
30:7	83
45:10	96
46:5	101

Jeremiah	
4:31	96
6:24	96
18:19	105
23:18-23	71

Ezekiel	
1:5	72
1:26	72
8:2	72
12:14	82
29:15	73
34:4	73
41:5	86
41:6	86
41:26	86

Daniel	
11:34	82
11:43	103

Hosea	
13:9	82

Joel	
2:17	101

Amos	
5:26	72

Micah	
4:10	96
6:4	125

NEW TESTAMENT

Luke	
2:36	126
8:35	62

Acts	
21:9	126

Romans	
13:14	121
16:7	126

1 Corinthians	
11:11-12	126
14	126
14:5	126
14:24	126
14:26	126
14:31	126
14:34-35	125
14:39	126

Galatians	
3:28	30, 126

Ephesians		*Colossians*		*1 Timothy*	
5	63	3:18	126	2:11-15	125, 126
5:22	126	3:19	126	2:11-14	125
5:25	126	4:1	121	3:2	126
6:9	121			3:12	126

Index of Authors

Alter, R. 74, 82
Angami, Z. 112
Ao, T. 30
Arnold, B. T. 64, 71

Barr, B. A. 52
Basumatary, S. 6, 19, 25, 26, 32–4, 46, 52
Bennett, J. M. 12, 13
Beyse, K.-M. 101
Bird, P. A. 65, 75–7
Brown, J. K. 119, 123
Brueggemann, W. 118, 123

Cassuto, U. 99
Clines, D. J. A. 65, 68, 72, 83, 101
Condren, J. C. 99
Cooper, T. T. 42

Daniel, K. 52
Dearman, J. A. 80
Dena, L. 33, 35–9, 42, 43, 52, 53
Donnemching, G. 9
Downs, F. S. 29, 32, 34, 39–42, 44–8, 50, 51, 53, 54, 112

Elwin, V. 42

Fee, G. D. 121
Fiorenza, E. S. 11
Foh, S. T. 97
Fretheim, T. E. 64, 71, 98

Grierson, G. A. 46
Gross, H. 103
Grudem, W. 84
Guite, M. 9

Hanghal, N. 81
Hangzo, T. M. 7, 31, 79

Hess, R. S. 97, 104
Hiebert, T. 73
Hminthanzuali 17, 18
Hnuni, R. L. 47, 54, 56, 113, 114
Holladay, W. L. 100

Jamir, S. 18, 26
Johnson, A. G. 13

Kamkhenthang, H. 7, 8, 10, 15, 16, 19, 20, 45, 55
Keitzar, R. 24, 112, 115
Key, A. F. 89
Khanna, S. K. 25, 26, 35
Khupkhothang 38
Kraus, H. 95, 99

Lalmuoklien 28, 52
Lambdin, T. O. 73
Lee-Barnewall, M. 87, 105
Liankhohau, T. 9, 21, 22, 30, 31, 46, 52
Lohr, J. N. 98
Lorrain, J. H. 47
Luai Chin Thang 14, 21–4

Macintosh, A. A. 98
Matskevich, K. 86, 87
Meyers, C. L. 11, 12, 96, 97, 100
Miller, P. 11, 12
Morris, J. H. 35, 44

Nembiakkim, R. 6
Ngaihte, S. T. 8, 52
Ngulzadal, S. 46

Ortlund, R. C., Jr. 67, 69, 79, 95, 98, 103
Otwell, J. H. 101

Phaipi, A. N. 7, 21, 22, 38, 59

Ralte, L. 49, 50
Ramsey, G. W. 88, 89
Ray, A. K. 8, 10, 43
Rodrigues, S. 8

Sarna, N. 71, 96
Savidge, F. W. 47
Schmitt, J. J. 101, 102, 104
Shakespear, J. 50
Shinkhokam. 9, 23
Siamkhum, Th. 15–18, 55, 56
Singh, K. M. 35, 39, 40
Singh, K. S. 20
Sparks, K. L. 121, 127
Speiser, E. A. 64
Stendebach, F. J. 72
Stuart, D. 121

Thangtungnung, H. 46
Thanzauva 47, 54, 56, 113, 114
Trible, P. 75, 82, 85, 97

Vogels, W. 97
Von Rad, G. 64, 65, 68, 74

Webb, W. J. 83, 85
Wenham, G. 71, 72, 80, 91, 96, 98
Wright, N. T. 117, 123, 124, 127

Zevit, Z. 82, 86, 90, 98, 99, 106
Zhimomi, K. 25, 26, 41

www.ingramcontent.com/pod-product-compliance
Lightning Source LLC
Chambersburg PA
CBHW061843300426
44115CB00013B/2488